ELITE
COMMUNICATION
SKILLS

— FOR —
YOUNG PROFESSIONALS

THE ULTIMATE GUIDE TO GET MORE RESPECT, MAKE YOUR
WORK LIFE EASIER, AND RAPIDLY ADVANCE YOUR CAREER

TY HOESGEN

AGI | ADVANCED
GROWTH
INSTITUTE

ISBN: 978-1-7781620-0-8 (Paperback)
ISBN: 978-1-7781620-1-5 (eBook)

To my partner, Liza
This book wouldn't exist without you.

To my parents, Jennifer and Robert
The author of this book wouldn't exist without you.

CONTENTS

YOUR FREE GIFT

THE INSTANT LIKABILITY ONLINE COURSE

How to Be Instantly Likable to Fast-Track Your Success
(While Still Being Your Authentic Self)

Research has revealed that, in addition to communication, **likability is actually more important than competence when it comes to being successful.**

Studies have shown that the more likable a person is, the more likely they are to <u>get promotions, pay increases, and see faster career jumps.</u>

If you improve your likability right from the start, everything you do with communication will automatically become easier.

In our *Instant Likability* course, you will discover:

→ 5 phrases that make you instantly more likable
→ The shockingly easy likability strategy anyone can use
→ The #1 word you should avoid at all costs

If you're interested in watching, I set up a page at www.instant-likability.com/free-access (QR code below) that allows readers of *Elite Communication Skills for Young Professionals* to **skip the $97 payment step.**

I'd like to give it to you as a gift of appreciation for reading this book. Your support really means a lot to me.

—Your biggest fan, Ty Hoesgen
Founder, Advanced Growth Institute

" *The one easy way to become worth 50 percent more than you are now—at least—is to hone your communication skills—both written and verbal.*

If you can't communicate, it's like winking at a girl in the dark—nothing happens. You can have all the brainpower in the world, but you have to be able to transmit it."

—Warren Buffet

I t's time. You have a meeting to go to.

You'd rather do the backstroke through hot coals than attend, but you don't have a choice. You might be able to get out of social interactions in your personal life, but at work—well, you can either do what needs to be done or try to find a job that requires *zero* human interaction.

No, you're better than that. You promise yourself you're going to speak up. You aren't going to sit there, body hunched over, trying to make yourself as invisible as possible.

This time, you're going to walk in with your head held high, and you're going to confidently share your ideas. You do your best to gulp down your nerves, take a deep breath, and start walking to the conference room.

Every step you take, the more the doubts start creeping in.

What if you stumble over your words?

What if you forget what you wanted to say?

What if people think your ideas are stupid?

As you get closer, your heart starts to pound in your chest. Your palms get clammy, and you're having difficulty swallowing past the lump in your throat.

By the time you walk into the room, you're terrified. All you can hear is the roar of blood rushing through your veins. You manage a few whispered greetings to your colleagues and look for a spot where you're least likely to get noticed.

As soon as you're seated, you hunch over and try to look busy to discourage others from talking to you.

Quietly, you watch your peers with admiration and a bit of envy. If only you could interact with others as easily as they do. If only you could stand up and speak with conviction. If only, if only, if only.

You know that your inability to communicate with people is holding you back in life, but what can you do? It's not like you can get a personality transplant.

And, anyway, is being able to communicate *that* important? Your mind goes back to thoughts of finding a different career—one where you don't need to interact with anyone. Ever. Like a...and that's where it all comes crashing down.

You have to communicate with people, no matter what job you have. Whether it's face-to-face, over the phone, in writing, or on video calls, every job requires communication skills.

Does that mean you're doomed to living in the shadows for the rest of your life?

Absolutely not. If you think your communication skills need work, you're in great company. Some of the most successful people in the world started as horrible communicators. We're talking ridiculously successful people—like Warren Buffet and Elon Musk.

Warren Buffet admitted to Gillian Zoe Segal in an interview for her book, *Getting There: A Book of Mentors*, that up until the age of 20, he couldn't speak in public. *"Just the thought of it made me physically ill,"* he said.

He decided to do something about it and invested $100 in a Dale Carnegie public speaking course. As part of the course, Buffet had to practice public speaking, which he continued to do even after it ended. He knew that if he didn't keep practicing, he'd fall back to his old ways. *"I just kept doing it, and now you can't stop me from talking!"* he said.

Why did Buffet invest in the course? Because he knew that the ability to communicate would be essential to all areas of his life. And he considers the Dale Carnegie certificate he earned to be the most important of his degrees.

Buffet explains, *"If you want to get ahead, focus on your communication skills."* He believes communication is so valuable that he recommends it as a top skill everyone should learn.

"The one easy way to become worth 50 percent more than you are now—at least—is to hone your communication skills—both written and verbal. If you can't communicate, it's like winking at a girl in the dark—nothing happens. You can have all the brainpower in the world, but you have to be able to transmit it," he told Michael Hood, a recent college graduate.

If you heard that Warren Buffet was talking about how to increase your worth, would you have expected him to be talking about improving your communication skills?

In an on-stage interview for Silicon Valley's Churchill Club, Elon Musk also admitted that he used to be *"horrendous at public speaking."* Not naturally extroverted, Elon would start shaking and find himself unable to speak. He knew he had to improve, so over time, he put in the work and *"learned not to do that."*

Even billionaire entrepreneur and founder of the Virgin Group, Richard Branson, says that *"Communication is the most important skill any leader can possess."* He credits much of Virgin's success to effective communication.

On his blog, Branson posted a list of his top ten quotes on communication. Coined by famous author Brian Tracy, one of these quotes is especially relevant: *"Communication is a skill that you can learn. It's like riding a bicycle or typing. If you're willing to work at it, you can rapidly improve the quality of every part of your life."*

So, if you're not the greatest communicator right now, it doesn't mean that you can't get better. You have the ability and opportunity in this very moment to work on your communication skills and transform your life. Armed with the proper knowledge, strategies, and techniques, anyone can improve their communication skills and enjoy success at a rapidly increased rate.

While developing your ability to communicate can be straightforward, it can be just as easy to make mistakes if you don't know what you're doing.

Take Jimmy Fallon's segment Hashtags as an example. Viewers share funny stories related to hashtags, and one of them is *#TextFail.* It shows communication misunderstandings caused by lack of context, basic incomprehension, and autocorrect.

Here are some messages that went terribly wrong:

- My friend texted me that they ran a mile in under 12 minutes. Instead of replying, *"Wow, you're fast!"* I sent, *"Wow, you're fat!"*

- My grandma thought *"LOL"* meant *"lots of love."* One time she sent, *"Headed to a funeral, LOL."*
- *"This isn't working out. We haven't been on the same page. I need to move on."* Sent to my boss instead of my girlfriend.

You might think these are funny. You might think these are cringeworthy. You might be thinking, "What kind of a monster breaks up with someone over text?"

These are entertaining examples, but more importantly, they show how easy it is for miscommunication to happen. And while double-checking your message to make sure you put an "s" in "you're fast" is important, communication goes far beyond this.

As you develop your communication skills, your life will change significantly. You'll find yourself getting more respect from everyone you meet. People will admire and look up to you like never before. Every interaction you have will become noticeably easier. You'll be better equipped to help others and offer your unique value to the world. You'll be in the best possible position to thrive.

The main goal of this book is to improve your communication skills right now—as fast as possible—so that you can rapidly advance your career and enjoy more success in your professional life. That being said, if you allow yourself to zoom out for a moment, your work life today could be just the tip of the iceberg.

As these communication skills become deeply ingrained in your mind, you will be able to apply them in *any* situation that involves other people—personally *and* professionally—and you'll be able to use them to your advantage for the rest of your existence.

If you're at a place in your life where you're not satisfied with your career, your relationships, or your finances, then read this book to the end and apply what you learn. It can change your life faster than you ever thought possible.

Let's get started.

CHAPTER 1

SET YOURSELF UP FOR SUCCESS

" No one can give you heart. No one can give you discipline. No one can make you unstoppable. Those are things you must decide for yourself.

But make no mistake, it's a decision. It's not a genetic gift. It's a mindset."

—**Tom Bilyeu**

A wkward and shy. Two words that used to describe my young self to a tee. Oh, and red. Definitely red. Every time I had to open my mouth, I'd turn beet red. It was not pretty.

Have you ever read something and thought, *"This sounds great, but I doubt it will work for ME"*? I used to think that way when I was first learning about communication. The mere thought of talking to someone made me sick to my stomach. I thought I was hopeless.

I grew up on a farm isolated from other kids, and I never had many friends. When it came to people skills, my older sister was the exact opposite of me.

She was outgoing and had a big personality. She often spoke for both of us. As a kid, whenever I was asked a question, my sister would jump in and answer for me before I had a chance to open my mouth.

I secretly enjoyed this. It meant I could avoid speaking and hide behind her. Unfortunately, this constant avoidance ended up being a major disadvantage for my future communication. I became so comfortable with not talking that when I did have to speak, the discomfort felt unbearable.

This continued into my teenage years and young adult life. I was fine interacting with certain family members and a few close friends, but I became extremely nervous and self-conscious when I needed to talk to anyone else.

I was decent at taking tests and writing papers, so I was able to get through university this way, but when I graduated and entered the professional world, things changed—big time. My first professional job was at an insurance agency, and my job was to sell life insurance, disability insurance, and critical illness insurance.

At the time, I often wondered why I subjected myself to such agony. Why would I pick a job where I had to talk about death and disease when asking someone about their weekend made me uneasy?

Well, in all honesty, I didn't have a choice. I applied to dozens of jobs, and this was the only offer that I got. And like most fresh college graduates, I needed the money.

I did think about running away to join the silent circus, but I didn't have any cool circus skills that would get me accepted. I also considered relocating to Antarctica. Penguins don't talk as much as humans, and I figured I'd have a better chance with them.

I ended up putting my penguin dreams on hold and starting my new Insurance Broker position. I had to interact with people constantly. I had to engage with clients, communicate with co-workers and bosses, speak in meetings, and deliver presentations.

It was my worst nightmare made reality. I lived in a perpetual state of anxiety, and every day was a struggle. I'd often stumble over my words or lose my train of thought altogether. So, I reverted to my childhood ways and tried to avoid talking as much as possible.

But this time, as an adult, there was no one answering questions for me. People expected me to be able to communicate. Sleepless nights became the norm as my fear of communicating with others intensified.

I learned two things very quickly:

1. **I knew absolutely nothing about communication.**
2. **I couldn't continue this way if I wanted to succeed in life.**

I would have to learn how to communicate to have *any* kind of professional success (or, at the very least, get to the point where I don't hate going to work so much.)

This is what started my journey. I decided then and there that I would conquer the dreaded beast. I became obsessed with improving my communication.

The next day, my life changed.

Just kidding. I wish I could say that. The truth is, after this desperate moment of realization, I still struggled for a long time. It was frustratingly hard to find quality resources, and having to figure a lot of things out on my own was often uncomfortable, embarrassing, and painful.

I spent many years and thousands of hours researching, reading, practicing, and experimenting to figure out what works and what doesn't. Over time, I eventually learned all of the best ways to optimize your communication. And I figured out the **easiest and fastest ways** to implement them and have success.

Once I finally nailed down a communication game plan and started following it, my life transformed dramatically.

I went from throwing up before meetings to calmly giving massive presentations on all aspects of communication. I went from being afraid to talk to a co-worker at the water cooler to confidently leading and managing teams. I went from working a low-paying job that I hated to owning a successful company and doing something that I love. I went from living with three roommates in small-town Saskatchewan (you may have to Google it) to living with the woman of my dreams in an 1800 sq. ft condo in downtown Toronto.

The goal of this story is not to impress you, but to *impress upon you* what's possible in your own life.

And anything is possible. When I first started writing communication guides for organizations, I watched countless employees transform their lives. Seeing how much these resources helped people planted a seed in my brain—a seed that would eventually grow into a burning desire to help people all around the world.

Flash forward, and my life is now dedicated to helping individuals and organizations across the globe improve their communication skills.

This book was created to save you time, get you faster results, and make your journey easier. You don't have to experience the pain that I did trying to figure everything out. You don't have to spend multiple thousands of hours reading every piece of communication content under the sun. Skip the years of struggle, confusion, and unnecessary work. You can read this book, implement what you learn, and enjoy the *massively positive impact* your new skills will have on your life.

With consistency and practice, even the most shy, nervous, and self-conscious people can overcome their struggles, make rapid improvements, and experience tremendous career and financial success. And if you're already a decent communicator, what you're about to read will skyrocket your life to the next level.

It starts with a shift in mindset. If you change your mindset first, you can make the entire process easier, more enjoyable, and ultimately make progress significantly faster.

THE EMPOWERED MINDSET OF THE LEARNER

Learning to communicate effectively is like learning to ski. You can read a million books about skiing, but if you never get your butt on a slope, you'll never learn to do it. And no, virtual skiing in your living room doesn't count (although with the wild advancements in VR, I may change my tune on this.)

To become an effective communicator, you need to practice in real-life situations with real human beings. Depending on where you're at in your journey, this could mean intentionally putting yourself in uncomfortable situations.

Adopting the empowered mindset of the learner—or learner's mindset—is one of the most powerful practices you can do to keep you going when things get difficult. Personally, I used to jump at the chance to quit something the second I was met with any resistance. When I finally learned to change my way of thinking, the resistance and discomfort became considerably more manageable.

So, what is the mindset of the learner?

UNDERSTANDING THE MINDSET

I'm a big fan of Tom Bilyeu, who co-founded Quest Nutrition and turned it into a billion-dollar brand. He's also the host of Impact Theory, one of my favorite podcasts.

Tom often talks about adopting the identity and mindset of the learner. The first time I heard him mention this concept, I had an epiphany. And it was a huge one, accompanied by swelling cinematic music like you'd hear in the final battle scene of a fantasy war movie. Epic moments aren't the same without equally momentous soundtracks.

As Tom explained the learner's mindset, I realized he was describing the perspective I had forced myself to adopt through years of struggle. To my delight, there was now a name for it and an extremely digestible way of teaching it to others. Much appreciated, Tom.

The learner's mindset is a shift in identity. Your sense of self is based on trying and learning, not succeeding and winning. You view your life as a stream of moments to practice and improve instead of obsessing over your performance and results. Every uncomfortable situation is now an opportunity to grow instead of a test that determines your self-worth. When you think this way, the pressure instantly drops.

This reduced pressure on yourself makes every tough situation less stressful. When you form your core identity around being a learner, the results don't matter. What matters is showing up to every interaction and applying the tips you'll read in this book.

The beauty of this mindset is that when you don't worry about results, you actually get far better ones. With less pressure, it will be easier to interact with others. You'll engage with a higher number of people and put in more communication reps simply because there's less resistance. Like any other skill, more reps = more results.

Many people don't think this way. You probably know a person who is constantly negative—they have no belief in themselves, and nothing ever works out for them. They've got that ongoing *"Woe is me"* vibe. And no matter how many times you tell them they can improve, they always find a reason why it won't work.

It's almost as if they're looking for reasons not to try. After all, if they're convinced they'll fail, why bother putting in any hard work in the first place?

It's okay if you feel that way yourself sometimes. We all have some version of that negative person living inside of us. The key is to not let them win, and consistently choosing the learner's mindset helps us do that.

As Tom explains it, humans are at the top of the food chain. And it's not because we're the strongest species—far from it. There are plenty of creatures out there stronger than us. We don't have claws or fangs to protect ourselves. We aren't the fastest species either.

What humans excel at, though, is adaptation. Tom points out that people frequently misquote Charles Darwin. He never said that the strongest specimens of a species survive. No, what Darwin said was, *"It is not the most intellectual of the species that survives; it is not the strongest that survives; but the species that survives is the one that is able best to adapt and adjust to the changing environment in which it finds itself,"* (Megginson, 1963).

And wow, we humans are excellent at adapting. We can adapt to and thrive in any environment, from the dry desert of the Sahara to the freezing cold of the Arctic. And it isn't just on a physical level.

We can adapt mentally. We can learn new skills, adopt new values, and pursue new things. What's even more extraordinary is how our thoughts can influence our physiology.

As Norman Doidge explains in his book *The Brain That Changes Itself,* you can rewire your brain with your thoughts. Your brain strengthens the neural connections it uses most, making it easier to believe the thoughts that you think frequently.

That's why things that you do all the time become easier and easier. Think about brushing your teeth. Do you have to think about what you're doing? Or do you just clean those pearly whites on autopilot?

Using this idea, you can rewire your brain to replace negative thoughts with positive beliefs and behaviors. You can replace putting yourself down with building yourself up. And the more you do it, the more your brain will default to empowering thoughts instead of negative ones that prevent you from taking action.

So, how do you put this into practice? How do you conquer the voice that keeps telling you you're not good enough?

DISCOVER THE IMPACT OF "YET"

Carol Dweck is a Stanford researcher and professor who wrote the book *Mindset: The New Psychology of Success.* Dweck introduced the world to the power of the word "yet."

The idea is to simply attach the word "yet" to a negative thought you're having. Every time you think you're not good enough, you add "yet." You're not good enough—*yet.*

Most of us understand that winning isn't permanent. If your favorite team wins today, you know that doesn't mean they're going to win tomorrow. Not without putting any effort in, and even then, there's no guarantee. We're pretty good at understanding that winning is a temporary state.

It can be easy to forget that failure and discomfort aren't permanent either. Just because you failed once doesn't mean you'll continue to fail. It's a temporary state, just like winning. And it can change quickly. You can fail big today and win big tomorrow.

Unfortunately, many of us have got it in our heads that failing makes us a failure, and that's what we'll be for the rest of our lives. We adopt and internalize an identity that has nothing to do with reality.

Instead of letting your insecurities and doubts win, remind yourself that failure is temporary by using the word "yet."

- You don't know how to confidently speak in meetings—yet.
- You don't feel comfortable in large group settings—yet.
- You haven't had much success on video calls with clients—yet.

"Yet" is possibly one of the most important words in the English language when it comes to shifting your mindset. This one word helps remind you that your situation is temporary.

More importantly, it reminds you that you are in control. You have the choice of staying as you are or getting better.

One problem I often hear is attributing things like "I'm not good enough" to external factors.

- I'm not good enough because I didn't get the right education.
- I can't talk to people because no one taught me how.
- I'm nervous around others because I was bullied as a child.

These can all be considered valid reasons, but the issue is that they take away your control. You can't go back and alter the past, and this way of thinking says you can't do anything about it because who you are now is who you will always be.

But is that really true? Of course not.

Let's take a simple example—the ability to drive a car. If you've ever driven a car, you were probably nervous when you first started driving on your own. But as time went by and you did it more and more frequently, it became second nature. Now, it's something you take for granted and can do without thinking.

I once watched a YouTube video of a person with no arms who learned how to drive. There was another video of someone with no legs who did the same. Pretty inspirational.

So, just like you can learn how to drive, and those amazing humans learned to drive despite their disadvantages, you can learn to do anything else you want to. As long as you *believe* you can. Your skills and abilities are now a result of the choices you make, which means that you have the power to change them and vastly improve whatever situation you're in.

And the more frequently you do something, the stronger those pathways in your brain become until, eventually, it becomes automatic.

You'll get in the habit of reminding yourself that you are a learner and that the journey is more important than the destination.

Tom's Bilyeu's take on this is gold. He says: *"I don't value being good at something; I value the pursuit of greatness. So I'm going to go pursue that, and oh yes, because I value that, I actually feel good about myself going after it. I don't feel badly about myself.*

I don't have any damage to my self-esteem when I fumble, and I'm super awkward—none of that hurts my self-esteem because what I value in myself, the very thing that I build my self-esteem around, is the pursuit. It's the willingness to accept I'm not good at it—yet—to remember that I'm a learner, that humans are the ultimate adaptation machine."

Now, it's time to put this into practice. Just like it would be hard to learn to drive without getting in a car, it's hard to shift to a learner's mindset without taking action. So, let's do a little exercise.

ACTION STEP

Remember those important pathways in your brain? By writing things down, you're training them to become stronger so your brain can change even faster.

Get out a piece of paper and a pen, and write out three communication areas where you think you're lacking and add the word yet. Here are some more examples:

- I'm not good at giving engaging presentations yet.
- I'm not good at asking powerful questions yet.
- I don't know how to write persuasive emails yet.

Once you've written three down, go back and highlight or underline the word **yet**. Really let it sink in. You are capable of improving at anything. If a person can drive with no limbs, you can definitely improve your communication skills.

THE THIEF OF JOY

Next, you're going to learn the final mindset shift needed to make your communication journey significantly easier and more enjoyable.

Simon Sinek often talks of two conferences he attended: one at Microsoft and one at Apple. At Microsoft, executives spent most of their time talking about what Apple was doing and how they could beat their rival.

At Apple, the executives spent all of their time talking about how they could improve *themselves* and better serve their customers.

After the Microsoft conference, Simon was gifted a Zune, Microsoft's answer to the iPod. This was back when MP3 players were still a thing. I remember spending hours downloading sick beats on LimeWire and then uploading them to my MP3 player to jam on the bus ride to school. It was a much simpler time.

Now, we have access to virtually every song ever created on a rectangle-shaped device that fits in our pockets and can be used anywhere. How wild is that? In my first draft of this book, I continued down this rabbit hole on technology and talked about how I believe every Black Mirror episode is going to come true, but my editor said it was "off-topic" and "unnecessary." Her feedback was slightly hurtful at first, but it was admittedly accurate. So, let's get back to the story.

According to Simon, the Zune was a great device. Slick and attractive with many more features than the iPod. The only drawback was that it couldn't connect to his iTunes account.

Later, when Simon was riding in a car with a high-level executive from Apple, he told the man about the Zune and pointed out that it was better than the iPod. The man shrugged and responded with a simple, "I know." And that was the end of the conversation.

Simon explains that Apple didn't care that the Zune was better than their iPod because the company didn't compare itself to Microsoft. Instead, the Apple team's focus was only on doing better than they did the day before. They always compared themselves to…themselves.

And that's why Apple was more successful than Microsoft. The iPod may not be around anymore, but that's because the iPhone replaced it. Microsoft's Zune went extinct with the dodo birds and was replaced by nothing.

What does all this have to do with changing your mindset to become a better communicator? Well, it reveals a prominent theme in our society.

We are taught to compare ourselves to others from an early age, and that behavior only gets reinforced as we get older.

Have you ever seen a frustrated parent demand that their child stops misbehaving and compare them to a better-behaved sibling? Have you heard a teacher praise their best students and treat them differently than the kids with lower grades? Or how about coaches telling their players they should be performing as well as the stars on the team?

It's a constant barrage of comparisons to other people until it almost becomes a reflex. You got a promotion. That's nice, but your friend Emily from college got a larger promotion six months before you. Your hair is the same length, but hers is real, and you have extensions. Oh, and she also just got engaged.

You got a new job with a substantial bump in salary. It feels good, but your cousin Brad is three years younger and still makes more than you. He barely works out anymore but can still squat, deadlift, and bench more than you can. And on it goes.

We've learned to measure our successes and failures based on other people, which inevitably leads to poor self-esteem, envy, and disappointment. No matter how successful you are, if you're always comparing yourself to others, it's hard to be truly happy achieving anything because there will always be someone better than you.

To make it tougher on ourselves, we rarely look beyond the surface. We don't ask ourselves how much work Emily put in to get that larger promotion six months earlier. We don't think about what Brad has done differently to have a higher income. We just assume it's something innate that we don't have.

The media plays a role in this as well. Advertisements are cleverly designed to take advantage of our insecurities, and they do it sneakily too. They never explicitly tell us we're not good enough, so you won't see an ad that says, *"Hey, you! You're not worthy of success, love, or happiness. But if you buy what we're selling, you will be! It's totally worth it!"*

Instead, they show us the life we could have if we buy their product or service. Everywhere you turn, from television and billboards to YouTube and Instagram, there's always an image of someone living a fantasy life that could be yours, but only if you buy into what they're selling.

In reality, you might feel better on a surface level for a brief period before eventually falling back into your usual comparison thoughts and behaviors. It's not your fault; that's the way your brain has been programmed through years of living in a culture of comparison.

If you're anything like me and the many professionals I work with, you want to develop powerful communication skills *while also* eliminating any stress and emotional turmoil caused by the idea that you're not good enough. And to do that, you're going to shift your comparison mindset.

CHANNEL YOUR INNER APPLE

Instead of comparing yourself to everyone else, channel Apple and forget about Microsoft. **Compare yourself to the person you were yesterday and strive to be better.** Just like Apple is always competing against Apple, you should always be competing against yourself.

By shifting your focus from other people to yourself, you will find it easier to stay motivated. You'll be happier throughout the entire learning process and more likely to stick with it until you get the results you want.

When you think about it, comparing yourself to other people doesn't even make sense. Even if you're the same age or have the same job, everything else is different. They have different parents and genetics, were raised differently, and their brains are wired differently. They've had experiences throughout their life that have shaped them into a very specific person—one who is entirely different from you.

Yet, despite logically knowing that you're different, you still put yourself on the same playing field just because of a few similarities.

Why is this so important? As you learn and develop the communication skills you need to fast-track your career growth, you may find that you become hyper-aware of other people's skills. And if you don't change your mindset now, it won't be long before you're comparing yourself to others more than ever before, which will diminish your progress in your mind and make it a lot tougher to keep going.

Because humans have such an innate desire to compare, I don't expect you to stop altogether. I still occasionally catch myself comparing to other people (mainly on Instagram), but now I know better than to linger in it and let it affect me.

You can do this too, and redirect your comparison energy in a healthy and productive way—**by comparing and competing with your past self. Specifically, your past self from the day before. Call this person "yesterday's you."** You can make it personal if you'd like and use your name. I compete against "yesterday's Ty."

Competing with yesterday's you is a game you can win every day, as long as you're taking some type of action to improve yourself.

If you spend 15 minutes every day reading this book, practicing what you learned, or analyzing how you communicated, you will improve every day. Doing a little bit every day will ensure that today's you will always be better than yesterday's you, and tomorrow's you will always be better than today's you. And the day after tomorrow's you—you got it.

I'll stop there, but if I were back in college writing an essay and trying to reach a certain length for the professor, I would definitely keep going. I would also increase the font size of the periods. It works surprisingly well. Too risky if you're submitting electronically, but virtually undetectable if you're handing in a printed copy.

If your life seems impossibly hectic and you're worried about a time commitment, I have good news. Everything you learn in this book has been designed for you to apply during your everyday life—to the things you are *already* doing—particularly in your workday. Because you're already interacting with people on a daily basis, even if you work from home, there are plenty of opportunities to practice what you're reading without setting aside a lot of extra time.

You could spend 5 minutes reading about emails or phone calls and pick two powerful tips that resonate with you. You could then practice those tips on every phone call or email you make throughout the day. If you approach your progress this way, you will repeatedly triumph over yesterday's you.

ACTION STEP

The next time you compare yourself to someone who seems super successful, whether in person or on social media, take a step back and reorient your thinking. Consider what you could still do on this day to ensure that today's you is better than yesterday's you. Do it immediately, or schedule it in your calendar and stick to it.

If you catch yourself comparing at the end of the day and you're thinking, "Ty, there's no more time to do anything," take a moment to look over what you've achieved that day. Try your best to find something you did to help you become even slightly better than yesterday. If nothing comes to mind, then it's the perfect time to commit to taking small steps tomorrow to make you a better communicator.

Don't forget, even a few minutes of reading and practicing counts!

If you start your journey by shifting your mindset to being an empowered learner and comparing yourself only to yesterday's you, you'll find your journey easier and much more enjoyable.

It will help with your mental toughness, and you'll be more likely to stay consistent on your path. This will allow you to learn the communication skills needed for your success at an even faster rate, and you'll be able to do so with significantly less resistance.

Game on, past self!

CHAPTER 2

BODY LANGUAGE

" *Your body language shapes who you are."*

—Amy Cuddy

When it comes to communication, most people first think of verbal or written language. In other words, we think of—well, words.

At the beginning of my professional life, I would constantly analyze my failed interactions. Could I have said something differently? Did I use the wrong words? Was there a better way to phrase what I said?

It was all about words. Over time, I discovered that there's a lot more to communication than the spoken word. Much of how humans communicate has little to do with words and lots to do with our bodies.

That's not to say words aren't important. One of my side hustles used to be teaching piano to young children, and I had a student by the name of Noah. Noah was a six-year-old boy with the attention span of a goldfish, and he loved to laugh at his own farts. Noah was one of my favorite students. One day, Noah stopped in the middle of a C major scale, looked over at me, and exclaimed:

> *"My brother says that if I keep playing the piano, I'm going to be a penis!"*

"Sorry, a what?" I asked, leaning in with great curiosity. *"A penis!"* he shouted, *"A penis, a penis!"* At that moment, it occurred to me that I was alone in a room with a six-year-old who was shouting the word "penis." I eventually realized he was trying to say the word "pianist," which actually made his statement accurate. A pianist is, indeed, a person who plays the piano.

So, the words you choose (and their pronunciations) do matter, but what you do with your body and face has an even greater impact on the way you communicate with others.

How much of an impact?

Studies show that our nonverbal cues make up a whopping 65-90% of our total communication (Crane & Crane, 2010).

Further research reveals that nonverbal signals have *four times* more impact on people's impression of you compared to the words you say (Goman, 2018).

That is why we're starting with body language. Improving your body language will have a tremendous impact on your career, and it can completely transform the way that everyone sees you and responds to you. In fact, there's a direct correlation between your body language and the amount of respect you get from others. Fortunately for us, these skills tend to be the easiest to practice and implement.

For example, speaking up in a meeting might be scary because people are guaranteed to notice you, but it's unlikely anyone will consciously recognize your change of body position and hand gestures.

THE POWER OF BODY LANGUAGE

The moment you step foot into a room, people immediately form an impression of you. They make snap judgments about your character and what type of person you are. These judgments are often made in a split second—before you even have the chance to open your mouth.

The majority of this impression is based on your body language—do you appear confident, professional, and capable? Or do you seem timid, nervous, and unsure of yourself?

If your body language and energy project confidence, people will be more inclined to give you the attention and respect that you deserve. If your body language gives off a vibe of awkwardness and insecurity, people may be quick to dismiss or discredit you. You could have the perfect script written for a presentation, but if it's delivered to an audience while slouching, looking down, and crossing your arms, your chance of success is extremely low.

There's also a close connection between your body language and how you feel. Think about your posture when you are happy and energetic (upright, shoulders back, head up) compared to when you are sad and stressed (slouching, hunched forward, head down). There's a big difference!

Some of us are not naturally confident people. And if you don't naturally feel confident when you're at work, your body language will likely match. If you're feeling doubtful, nervous, or even a bit unsure of yourself during a meeting, you may unconsciously be showing it by the way you're sitting—reinforcing everyone's perception of you not being as self-assured or capable as you should be.

While our emotions and thoughts influence our posture, it also works in reverse. You can alter your body language to improve your mood and state of mind.

Try this: hunch forward with your arms crossed, legs together, and lower your chin to your chest, looking down at the ground. Stay here for 5 seconds. How do you feel?

Now, sit upright with your back straight, shoulders down and back, arms at your sides, legs comfortably open. Lift your chin and tilt your head up slightly, looking straight ahead. Stay here for 5 seconds. How do you feel now?

This quick exercise demonstrates how the position of your body sends direct signals to your brain about how you're feeling and functioning.

Communication is much easier when you feel good and you're in the right state of mind. When you're feeling down, you might prefer to square off against a pack of rabid wolves than talk to another human. And if you're an introvert, interacting with other people can be challenging at the best of times, let alone when you aren't "feeling it."

But how do you change your mood? According to Tony Robbins, a legend in the self-development world, one of the quickest ways to change your state is through your body and physiology. *"Motion creates emotion,"* he says.

For example, it's difficult to stay upset if you stand up, put your arms up in the air, and start laughing. Even if you're not feeling it at first, these motions will eventually cause the positive feeling to become real.

This isn't a new idea, either. In the classic 1893 book *Psychology*, William James stated, *"What kind of an emotion of fear would be left if the feeling neither of quickened heart-beats nor of shallow breathing, neither of trembling lips nor of weakened limbs, neither of goose-flesh nor of visceral stirrings, were present, it is quite impossible for me to think…I say that for us emotion dissociated from all bodily feeling is inconceivable."*

Now that you have a better understanding of the connection between your body and emotions (along with some new words from William James to use in your next Valentine's Day poem), let's dive into how to change our physiology to optimize our communication.

POWERFUL POSTURE

Do you ever find yourself slouching? How often do you hunch forward and stare at your phone? Have you ever pretended to look down at your phone in a social setting because it felt awkward to look up?

I used to do this a lot. This "closed" posture was one way I tried to hide from the world. It was my version of the camouflage abilities a chameleon possesses. I might not have been able to change the color and pattern of my skin to blend into the background—although I've tried many times—but I would do the human equivalent and make myself as small as possible.

Blending into the background works well for chameleons in nature, but it doesn't work in the business world. Well, not if you want to get ahead. And especially not if you want massive amounts of success.

Trying to blend in and go unnoticed in your professional life projects a lack of confidence. Luckily, even if you don't have that Rihanna or ASAP Rocky level of confidence yet, you can still use your body to project confidence in a way that makes others respect and listen to you.

How do you do this?

When you're *standing*, make sure your back is straight, push your shoulders down and back, open up your chest, and keep your head up. Have your hands visible at your sides. Make sure that you're taking up adequate space and standing with your feet a confident distance apart—wider than shoulder-width. If this width feels too weird for you, at least stand a couple inches wider than you normally do.

When you're *sitting*, adopt a relaxed but open position. Just like standing, keep your shoulders back and your posture straight, even if you're leaning against the back of a chair. Again, keep your hands visible. Place them on the arms of your chair or on top of the desk or table. We'll look in-depth at why visible hands are so important near the end of the chapter.

Avoid closing your body language by crossing your arms, hunching over, or holding objects like bags or notebooks directly in front of you. It gives the impression that you're trying to protect yourself, implying fear rather than confidence.

Additionally, closed body language can make people think you aren't sincere or don't know what you're talking about. You could be the foremost expert on a topic, but people won't listen to you if your posture is timid and unsure.

To make sure you're not giving off the wrong impression, you should also be mindful of the angle of your body in relation to the person you're speaking to. We tend to turn our bodies subconsciously to where our mind wants to go. So, if you're nervous during a conversation and escape is on your mind, you may angle your body towards the door without realizing it.

Even if you're not aware of it yourself, it's been shown that our brains tend to pick up on this nonverbal cue when we see it in another person. That means angling away from someone can signal your disinterest in speaking to them, and they might perceive you as rude. This is fine if you're at a party and a stranger is talking your ear off, but not ideal when you're trying to build professional relationships. If you keep your shoulders and torso turned toward your conversation partner, you'll look engaged and interested in what they have to say, which will help you make faster and stronger connections.

Adopting a consistently strong posture is essential because it gives the impression of self-assurance, high energy, and authority. This is one of the simplest and most underutilized ways to help others view you as a leader.

ACTION STEP

Get in the habit of using your new powerful posture as much as possible. Make sure you're sitting or standing confidently throughout your day—especially when other people are around.

At first, it might feel odd and unnatural. You'll probably find yourself reverting to your usual positions until it becomes more familiar. This is to be expected. Many of us have terrible posture from hunching over our phones and computers all day, so your muscles likely aren't used to this enhanced body language.

Fortunately, it doesn't take long to adjust, and this posture will feel more natural each time you do it. It will soon become part of your routine, and you'll find your body automatically goes to a position that's both comfortable and confident.

Of course, you don't have to sit like this 24/7. If you like to sit in a "gangsta lean" type of posture every so often while crushing Netflix, I would never take that away from you. Just keep in mind that the more consistent you are, the quicker it will become a habit.

If you often find yourself forgetting about your posture, put a small sticky note next to your computer and any other place you spend a lot of time working. Use the sticky notes as little visual cues to remind you to sit up straight with your shoulders down and back. I would keep one by my workspace to remind me throughout the day and another one tucked discreetly in my notebook to remind me during meetings.

> When you see the sticky note and adjust your posture, remind yourself that you should be sitting in a strong, confident position because that's who you are—a strong, confident person. If that seems too cheesy and far-fetched for you right now, you can tell yourself that's who you *will* be. You will get there, even if you're not there *yet*.

You don't even have to write anything on the sticky notes. "Confident body language" written on a little piece of bright neon paper might invite questions. No one will know what a blank sticky note means, but you will, and that's all that matters.

This is an incredibly effective hack to change the way you feel and how others treat you.

By regularly using powerful posture, you will gain two incredible benefits:

1. **You will consistently find yourself in a better mood, feeling more confident in every situation, and having more energy.**
2. **Others will take you more seriously, listen closely to your ideas, and respond more positively to you.**

TALK WITH YOUR HANDS

Remember that popular phrase from the 1990s, *"Talk to the hand"*? It was a dismissive way of telling someone that you weren't interested in what they were saying. Sassy teens seemed to enjoy this phrase, particularly when they added, *"Cause the face ain't listening."*

Oddly enough, with just a small adjustment to that phrase, you get a compelling technique that makes people pay more attention to you. Talking *with* your hand (well, hands) has been proven to engage your listeners substantially more than keeping them still.

Vanessa Van Edwards—the founder of Science of People and author of *Captivate: The Science of Succeeding with People*—researches human behavior, communication, and relationships. She conducted a fascinating study attempting to discover what sets viral TED Talks apart from less popular ones.

The study consisted of 760 volunteers who watched hundreds of hours of TED Talks and subsequently rated the videos. Vanessa discovered that **the volunteers who watched the videos *on mute and without subtitles* rated the videos *the same* as those who watched the videos *with sound*.** She always knew body language was important, but this proved that nonverbal communication has more impact on an audience's perception of a speaker than anything else.

The study also found that the biggest difference between the highest and lowest-rated TED Talks was *the average number of hand gestures*. The speakers in the highest-rated videos with an average of 7.3 million views used 465 hand gestures on average. Conversely, those in the lowest-rated videos with an average of 124,000 views used 272 hand gestures on average. The lower-rated and less watched videos had 41.5% fewer hand gestures.

While quantity mattered, the type of gestures they used was also important. As Vanessa explains, *"The best speakers used congruent gestures. Those were gestures that added meaning or depth to words. If a TED speaker said they had a big idea, they held their hands out wide like carrying a heavy load. If a speaker said they had three ideas, they held up three fingers."*

She cautions that while gestures can improve comprehension and help with charisma and fluency, they can also backfire. Too much gesturing can make you seem fake. Instead, she advises people to watch videos of themselves when speaking to see where they normally add gestures and then dial it up a notch.

Another important difference between popular and less popular TED Talks was how much the speaker smiled, regardless of the seriousness of the topic. The more the speaker smiled, the more views the video received.

Vanessa admitted that this discovery helped her become a better speaker. *"In the past, I thought if I'm speaking about a serious topic, I'd better look serious,"* she explained. *"Now I know we always want something to smile about, and a little bit of laughter helps with retention and learning."*

THE PSYCHOLOGY BEHIND HAND GESTURES

Using hand gestures while talking might seem like a personality quirk. After all, not everyone does it. Or do they?

As it turns out, humans are born talking with our hands, and this can affect our ability to use language. Researchers discovered that at 18 months old, the infants who used more gestures developed better language abilities. This has led many people to believe there's a correlation between hand gestures and intelligence level—that is, the more you talk with your hands, the more intelligent you are.

Further proof that humans were born to use hand gestures was found by Spencer Kelly, associate professor of psychology and co-director of the Center for Language and Brain at Colgate

University. He discovered that even blind people use hand gestures when talking to other blind people.

Kelly also found that people listen more closely when you use hand gestures because they encourage people to listen to the deeper acoustics of speech. His research has led him to believe that gestures may be a fundamental part of language instead of just a supporting act.

More studies have shown that gesturing plays a role during the memory encoding process. Using them helps our brain form lasting memories and store information. They also increase our retention and make it easier to access memories. Oddly enough, retention and recall improve even more when the speaker *cannot see* their own gestures. This indicates that the movements themselves are responsible for improving memory rather than the visual cues (Cook, Yip, & Goldin-Meadow, 2010).

Beyond memory, gesturing has been shown to enhance understanding as well. A study discovered that encouraging children to gesture while explaining solutions to math problems helped them think of new and correct problem-solving strategies (Broaders, Cook, Mitchell, & Goldin-Meadow, 2007).

To recap, gesturing helps:

- **People pay more attention to what you're saying**
- **Create charisma and fluency**
- **Improve memory formation and recall**
- **Expand problem-solving abilities**

KEEP IT IN THE BOX

While thinking outside the box is encouraged, gesturing outside the box is not. The box I'm referring to is the safe zone for hand gestures. It starts at the top of your chest and ends at hip level, and it extends a few inches to the right and left of your arms. Just imagine a really big present in front of you, and keep your hands and arms within that present box.

If you gesture outside the box, you could be seen as lacking control, and people will find it distracting. They'll end up focusing on your gestures rather than what you're saying.

COOL, PALM, AND COLLECTED

The position of your palms can significantly influence how people react to you. Allan Pease, an Australian expert on body language and author of over 20 books, demonstrated this fact in a TED Talk.

He repeated a set of instructions three times. The first time, he gestured with his palms facing upwards. When he repeated them the second time, his palms were facing down. The third time, he pointed with his forefinger. After each round, he asked the audience how they felt about his instructions.

The first time with his palms up, people were drawn to him and were far more willing to cooperate. The second time with his palms down, they felt like he was giving them orders and weren't as likely to comply. With the finger points in the third round, people were extremely resistant because his instructions had moved from orders into what felt like authoritarian territory.

A similar study showed that audiences spoken to with palms up gestures retained up to 40% more of the information presented than the palms down and finger-pointing groups. They also found the speaker to be more friendly, open, and trustworthy.

The audience where the speaker used finger-pointing had the lowest level of retention, and they also used the worst adjectives to describe the speaker. Finger-pointing can indicate that you're upset and losing control of a situation, and for many people, it brings to mind playground bullies and being scolded by parents. That's certainly not a feeling you want your audience to associate you with.

So, keep those palms up! It's the best way to gesture to connect with people, get them to listen and cooperate with you, and have them think positively of you.

ACTION STEP

Make a point—but not a literal point, as we just learned—to add more hand gestures when you're speaking. As you use them more, you'll find moving those hands improves your speaking and helps your thoughts flow more freely.

It can be valuable to make a note of others' gestures as well. I don't believe anyone has copyrighted hand gestures, so observe how your favorite speakers use them and steal any ideas you like.

SHOW ME YOUR HANDS

If you keep your hands hidden all the time, people tend not to trust you. This is a natural reaction resulting from our human survival instinct. Once upon a time, our ancestors relied on visual details to make survival decisions.

When someone approached with their hands hidden, it indicated possible danger. Alternatively, someone approaching with their hands in plain view was less likely to have evil intentions and more likely to be viewed as trustworthy.

While our world has changed, and this suspicion of hidden hands is no longer necessary for our everyday survival, the instinct is a part of our biology that has remained over time. Interestingly enough, we still have many of the same instincts as our prehistoric ancestors. As you make your way through this book, you'll discover more about them and their effects on various aspects of our modern communication.

As you'll recall from earlier in the chapter, it's beneficial to keep your hands visible as much as possible. Doing so ensures that you're not putting yourself at a disadvantage from a trust and relationship-building perspective.

When standing, it's best to keep your arms resting at your sides. When I first learned about this, I tried hard to make the change, but it was oddly difficult. I used to find great comfort in keeping my hands buried deep inside my pockets, and they rarely left those trouser safe havens if I was around other people. For some reason, it was almost painfully uncomfortable to initially keep them out in the open.

I felt like Ricky Bobby in Talladega Nights when he's getting interviewed and can't stop awkwardly raising his hands.

> Ricky: "I'm not sure what to do with my hands."
> Reporter: "Uh, you can just hold them down by your side. Yep. Great."

The second option is to put your hands in the steeple position. The steeple position is when you hold your palms facing each other, with the fingertips of one hand lightly touching the fingertips of the other, forming what looks like a church steeple. This is a popular hand position among leaders, as it has been shown to both inspire confidence inside you and project it to those around you.

If you find it hard to keep your hands still, steepling gives them something to do and can be a great way to control your fidgeting. Just make sure not to drum your fingers together; this makes you look like an evil genius devising a master plan to take over the world.

One gesture you want to avoid is the "fig leaf," which involves one hand cupping over top of the other and resting in the region of your groin. Though many people use it, it projects weakness and insecurity.

Remember, your hands should also be visible when sitting. Avoid hiding them in your lap or under the table. It's best to rest them on the arms of your chair or the surface in front of you. You can also use the steeple when sitting as a power pose for your hands. If you ever watch the show *Shark Tank*, you'll see Kevin O'Leary use the steeple when he's seriously considering taking a deal.

EYES, EYES, BABY

Eye contact plays a significant role in communication. Knowing how to make eye contact the right way is one of the easiest ways to strengthen your relationships with others, which is incredibly valuable. If you have a stronger relationship with your boss, you're more likely to get promoted or get a raise. If you have a stronger relationship with your co-workers, they're more likely to get along with you, listen to you, and help you when you need it.

To some people, eye contact comes easily. To others, not so much. If you're part of the latter group, that's perfectly normal—eye contact can be super intimidating for many of us. Prolonged eye contact can feel like undressing in front of a crowd while wearing your least favorite underwear. It can make us feel uncomfortable and exposed.

There could be many reasons for this. It could be intimacy issues, shyness, not enough confidence, or simply a lack of experience. Fortunately, eye contact is a skill that anyone—yourself included—can learn and master.

Using the right amount of eye contact makes people perceive you as:

- **Charming and likable**
- **Trustworthy and believable**
- **Intelligent and competent**
- **Confident and emotionally sound**

Another advantage is that you'll make a longer-lasting impression. When you don't make eye contact, people subconsciously dismiss you and don't consider what you have to say as important. When you wield the power of eye contact effectively, people are far more likely to remember you and what you have to say.

Just like using powerful posture, eye contact makes you seem more confident and assertive. You project an aura of courage and high self-esteem when you're able to hold eye contact with someone. A person with more self-esteem will break eye contact less frequently than someone with lower self-esteem. Breaking eye contact and constantly looking down or around the room can make you appear submissive and nervous, which means you're less likely to get respect and establish a connection.

Of course, that doesn't mean you should start a staring contest without telling the other person. Too much eye contact can cross over into overly intense or creepy territory.

THE RIGHT WAY TO USE YOUR EYEBALLS

Here are some general tips for you to maximize the effectiveness of your eye contact:

- Start making eye contact **from the beginning**, even before you start talking.
- Make eye contact approximately **60-70% of the time** during a conversation (personally, I like to be on the higher side).
- Use the **triangle technique**: imagine an upside down triangle on the person's face that connects their eyes to their mouth. Their two eyes and their mouth are each a point on the triangle. Instead of looking away fully, you can move your gaze from one of the triangle's points to another point every five seconds.
- When it's time to break eye contact, don't suddenly dart your eyes away. Instead, **look away slowly**. If you move your eyes too quickly, it makes you seem shy or nervous.
- **Looking down** when breaking eye contact can make you seem **insecure**, while **looking up** can strengthen your energy and make you appear **curious and deep in thought.** Looking up also keeps you more open to receiving the other person's energy.
- When speaking to a group, **pick one person at a time to focus on.** Choose one person to look at when explaining a thought, and then switch to another person when you start a new sentence. Make sure that you keep an even rotation and make eye contact with everyone in the group.

If you're finding this new amount of eye contact really uncomfortable, I've got a great *eye-dea* for you (couldn't resist).

The reason you're uncomfortable is that you don't like looking directly into the eyes themselves. So, look at the space on their face between their eyes instead. Unless you're almost nose to nose with someone, it's impossible for them to tell exactly where you're looking. Looking at the space between their eyes looks like you're making eye contact and will still give you the benefits, but it doesn't have the same intimacy that makes you uncomfortable. And your conversation partner will be none the wiser.

Test this with a friend or family member you feel comfortable with. Sit a normal distance away from them and try looking at different spots on each other's faces. See how far away from their eyes you can get before they can tell you're no longer making eye contact. How far did you get?

RESTING WITCH FACE?

Science has proven that every one of the seven basic emotions humans experience—anger, disgust, contempt, fear, happiness, sadness, and surprise—has a facial expression associated with it. The close tie between facial expressions and emotions means that they tend to be unconscious and involuntary.

Now, that doesn't mean you can't learn to control your facial expressions. Especially in professional settings, it's important that your face matches the message you're trying to send.

Let's say you've come up with a creative new idea to generate more leads for your organization. You're pumped to share your idea, but instead of looking excited, your face looks cold and stern. These mixed signals will leave your team feeling confused and unsure of both you and your idea.

Fortunately, it's easier to control your facial expression if your body language already represents the message you're trying to convey. If you've followed the body language tips laid out earlier and positioned yourself in a way that looks strong and confident, most of the time, your facial expression will match.

I say most of the time because some of us have resting faces that don't always give off the impression that we'd like. There's a famous one that rhymes with "resting witch face" that is best left at home when you're trying to make a positive impact. Thankfully, it's possible to train yourself to adopt more appropriate facial expressions, and it starts by gaining awareness and then making the necessary adjustments.

ACTION STEP

Usually, I don't recommend staring at yourself on the screen during a virtual meeting (more on this in the chapter on video calls). However, it is an easy way for you to quickly check on the facial expressions you're sporting, especially the face you have while you're listening. Check your facial expression every so often on virtual meetings to make sure you don't look like someone who just stubbed their toe.

When you know you're on camera, you're less likely to make faces that will put other people off. That's why asking for help from a friend or trusted co-worker can help you even more. Just say something along the lines of, *"Hey, I'm learning about the power of body language and facial expressions. Can you watch my facial expressions over the next few days and tell me what you notice?"*

If you ask someone who knows you very well, they may already have an answer. When I asked someone close to me several years ago, they didn't hesitate to say, *"You look VERY stern whenever I see you working on your computer. Or in meetings, when I can tell you're thinking hard about something. If I didn't know you, I'd think you were cold and unapproachable. You look way too intense."*

At this point in my life, having already spent many years working on my people skills, I learned that while I was usually smiling and looking happy when talking with others, I gave the exact opposite impression when I wasn't speaking. Now, whenever I know there are people around, I do my best to keep a lighter facial expression, a less furrowed brow, and sometimes even a slight smile to maintain my warm, approachable energy.

If I hadn't made a point to learn this, I would still be projecting unintentional cold signals to the people around me. And because first impressions are so important, imagine the effects that a negative facial expression could have on a future client, boss, or partner's perception of you.

As we wrap up this chapter, how are you feeling about body language? You just learned how to position your back, chest, shoulders and feet for open, powerful posture, you learned about hand gestures and keeping your hands visible, you learned the best ways to use eye contact, and you learned to be mindful of your facial expressions.

You may find that some of these changes feel awkward and unnatural at first. However, once you know what to do with your body and start implementing these tips regularly, it will all become habitual. The beauty of body language is that it doesn't involve any advanced skills or complicated strategies to change. All it takes is awareness and repetition. It won't be long before you don't even have to think about your body language anymore, and it will all come naturally.

As you develop these nonverbal communication skills, you'll notice others treating you with significantly more respect and taking you more seriously than ever before. People will start seeing you as a high-level professional before you even say anything—putting you at a major advantage in every situation.

CHAPTER 3

SPEAKING UP

" *You have to speak your mind and do the stuff that makes you laugh."*

—Joe Rogan

Meetings used to scare me to death. Well, maybe not to death, but usually to the point of sickness. I remember running to the bathroom to hide before meetings and throwing up because I was so nervous.

I wish I could say I was like Hockey Hall of Fame Goalie Glen Hall, who would get so stressed before games that puking became part of his pre-game ritual. The difference is that Hall would always show up ready to perform, and he played his heart out every night. At this stage of my career, I couldn't even work up the courage to open my mouth.

Glen Hall is known as one of the best goalies of all time and picked up the nickname "Mr. Goalie." Ty Hoesgen, in his younger days, was known as quiet and fearful, and the only nickname he had was "Mr. Nervous." Writing in the third person aside, throwing up before meetings wasn't ideal, especially since I was desperately trying to pack on muscle to increase my self-esteem.

Using the techniques I'll share in this chapter, combined with the mindset and body language strategies from Chapters 1 and 2, I was able to work through the hiding, puking, and staying silent during meetings. Now, I'm just as comfortable talking to a small group of ten as a stadium of ten thousand. I also haven't puked in years, which has been much more effective for muscle gain.

I'm telling you this not to show off, but to show you what's possible in your own life. It's okay if you're not naturally inclined to share your thoughts and speak up in meetings. Just because it doesn't come effortlessly doesn't mean you can't change and become excellent at it.

My transformation didn't happen overnight, and it would be unrealistic to expect your growth to be any different. If you take small steps every single day and focus only on competing with yesterday's you, you'll be amazed by the person you will become.

TRANSFORMERS

As Warren Buffet mentioned in the introduction, you could be a genius, but if you can't communicate, it's like winking at someone in the dark—nothing happens. What's even worse than these dark winks? Staying silent at work. It completely undermines your potential and prevents you from expanding your reach, getting noticed, and having other people recognize your full value.

Speaking up might be scary at first, but the more you open up and share your ideas, knowledge, and perspectives, the more free you will feel in your everyday life. It's truly liberating.

Additionally, you might be doing your organization a disservice by not providing ideas that could lead to meaningful innovation and boost everyone's success. And before you say that you have nothing to contribute, remember that even the wildest ideas can spark something new and valuable.

For example, think of the Transformers franchise. It began with someone thinking:

> *"What if our cars weren't just cars…what if our cars were also…robots?"*

This thought turned into thousands of action figures, and then someone came up with the idea of turning them into a cartoon, which worked so well that Transformers became much more than a toy line.

Over the decades, there have been multiple cartoon series, comic books, and blockbuster movies (the 2007 movie is the reason I have a lifetime crush on Megan Fox, even if she drinks blood as a symbol of love.) Transformers has made Hasbro and their partners billions of dollars, and it all started with a simple question, *"What if our cars were also...robots?"*

So, before you go dismissing your ideas as being unworthy of saying out loud, think about Transformers. Think about how a thought that could've come from the minds of two teenagers hot-boxing a Pontiac Sunfire ended up being worth billions of dollars. And let those ideas flow.

WHY DON'T WE SPEAK UP?

Despite the benefits of speaking up, research from Fierce Conversations and Quantum Workplace shows that approximately 50% of employees rarely say what's on their minds, whether they're talking to colleagues or managers. Furthermore, a Vital-Smarts report showed that 37% of employees don't speak up because they're afraid it could hurt their career prospects or people would think they complain too much. Another 45% were concerned that their co-workers wouldn't support them. What's the cause of this?

Just like our suspicion with hidden hands, our old caveman survival instincts play a significant role in this way of thinking. When we lived outdoors and had to hunt for our food, we had a greater likelihood of survival if we were part of a group. More people hunting meant more opportunities to get food. Sticking together in a group also meant a lower chance of being targeted by predators and a higher chance of being able to defend ourselves.

So, our instincts are to do what we can to be accepted by the tribe. As organizational anthropologist Judy E. Glaser writes, people avoid speaking up because we don't want to be rejected. We fear that rejection could lead to isolation or ostracization from the group. And due to our instincts, we consider this a fate that could result in our demise.

Consciously, we know that we won't die if people disagree with what we say. It's not as if being given the cold shoulder at work means that we'll never be able to eat again, or we'll end up being devoured by a pack of wolves because we're no longer in a group. However, our instincts are so deeply ingrained that we still associate rejection with a lower chance of survival in our subconscious mind. This is one of the main reasons so many of us are terrified of speaking up.

It's also not unusual to be intimidated by other people in a meeting, especially if we think they're well beyond us in experience and knowledge. There's also the matter of certain people being more verbally dominant than others. According to Susan Cain in her book *Quiet: The Power of Introverts in a World That Can't Stop Talking,* three people do 70% of the talking in an average meeting. And as a result, many people don't get to share simply because they can't get a word in edgewise.

You may avoid speaking up for one or more of these reasons. It could also be due to something that happened in your past. Take a moment and reflect on what the reason is for you. The best way to overcome a challenge is first to gain awareness of the cause.

SHIFT YOUR FOCUS TO OTHERS

One way to make speaking up in meetings easier is to take the spotlight off yourself and think more about helping others. This is an approach that many professionals use to gain the courage they need to use their voice. Instead of thinking that it's all about voicing your opinions and standing out, shift your focus onto the benefits for everyone else in the meeting.

When you hold back because you think your idea isn't good enough, or you don't want to share a thought that isn't fully formed, consider that you could be the cause of someone else's breakthrough.

If you catch yourself thinking, "It's not my place," understand that keeping quiet is not the best thing for your team. By withholding anything that could benefit your organization, you could be causing future harm to the people you work with—creating extra work, headaches, and struggles.

This perspective doesn't resonate with everyone, but if you support the Utilitarian "greatest good for the greatest number" way of thinking, this may be exactly what you need to help break through.

Certain people find it difficult to speak up when it's all about themselves, but when it's about contributing to a collective goal and sharing a purpose with their fellow humans, they're able to overcome their fears and start making steps towards change.

With all of the self-centered, "look at me" attitudes in modern society, shifting your focus away from yourself will set you apart. It might seem counterintuitive, but focusing less on yourself will actually help you stand out from the competition. The employees whose main focus is to help the organization succeed are often the most respected and valued in the workplace, and this focus delivers extraordinary results.

To ensure none of this work goes unnoticed, we have an entire chapter later in the book dedicated to increasing your visibility in the workplace. There are nine strategies for you to utilize that will make sure everyone in the company knows exactly how valuable you are. That way, when it comes time for new opportunities, raises, and promotions, you'll be the first one on their mind.

THE ELITE RELAXATION TOOL

So, how did I eventually learn to calm my nerves, reduce my anxiety, and stop throwing up before meetings?

After many sleepless nights and hours of research, I finally discovered a tool that would end up radically changing my life. I could use it in literally any situation—anytime, anyplace, anywhere. And it was absolutely free. It was almost too good to be true.

You have this tool on you right now. In fact, you never leave home without it.

This remarkable, life-changing tool is none other than your *breath*.

Research has proven that there is a strong correlation between the way you breathe and the way you think and feel. Intentional breathing is one of the fastest, easiest, and most effective ways to change your thoughts and emotions.

Let's explore three powerful breathing techniques that will help you relax and calm your nerves before a meeting, important event, or any time you're feeling stressed or anxious.

As you use them, you will find yourself in a more relaxed, elevated state of mind, which will naturally boost your confidence, allow you to think more clearly, and make it significantly easier to speak up.

BOX BREATHING

Box breathing is a breathing technique used to relieve stress, and it comes highly recommended by the U.S. Navy SEALs.

Mark Divine, former U.S. Navy SEALs Commander, says, *"Box breathing allowed me to perform exceedingly well in the SEALs. It was instrumental in saving my life several times in crises. I was able to remain calm and focus clearly to avoid reactionary thinking, or worse, panic."* Here's how to do it:

1. Inhale slowly through your nose for 4 seconds
2. Hold your breath for 4 seconds
3. Exhale slowly (nose or mouth) for 4 seconds
4. Hold your breath for 4 seconds

On your inhales, allow your stomach to rise and expand as your lungs fill up with air. On your exhales, let your stomach fall as your abdomen muscles gently contract. Repeat the full cycle until you feel focused and relaxed.

Box breathing was the first type of intentional breathing that I learned about. I was quite the pessimist at this time, but I still remember thinking, *"Hey, if this works for the Navy SEALs, there's no way it won't work for me. My problems are peanuts compared to what they have to deal with."*

The very next day, I decided to give it a try. I stood in the office bathroom, nauseous as ever, staring at myself in the mirror. *"In, 2, 3, 4, hold, 2, 3, 4, out, 2, 3, 4, hold, 2, 3, 4."*

After forcing myself to focus through a couple of rounds of breath, a smile crept across my face. I actually felt pretty good. The nausea was still there, but I was definitely keeping my food down today. I left the bathroom still grinning, feeling like a divine being who had just tapped into some New Age sorcery. From that day forward, I never threw up before a meeting ever again.

THE PHYSIOLOGICAL SIGH

The physiological sigh was popularized by Andrew Huberman, Stanford neuroscientist and host of the Huberman Lab Podcast, one of my all-time favorites. Huberman believes it's one of the best real-time tools people can use to reduce stress throughout their day. Here's how to do it:

1. Deep inhale through your nose
2. Add another inhale through your nose, but shorter this time
3. Extended exhale through your mouth

That's two consecutive inhales through the nose (one long, one short) followed by one long exhale through the mouth. The duration of your exhale should be longer than your two inhales. If you want, you can repeat it a second or third time, but typically one or two physiological sighs are all you need.

This is my go-to breathing exercise if I start feeling stressed or anxious and need to calm down *fast*. It's super quick and effective, and even if you're surrounded by people (like frustrating co-workers) you can still pull it off silently without anyone noticing.

"Don't control your thoughts with your thoughts. Use your body," Huberman says.

4-7-8 BREATHING

The 4-7-8 breathing technique was created by Dr. Andrew Weil, who refers to it as a *"natural tranquilizer for the nervous system."* Here's how to do it:

1. Inhale through your nose for 4 seconds (make sure your mouth is closed)
2. Hold your breath for 7 seconds
3. Exhale through your mouth for 8 seconds

When you're exhaling, close your lips into a small "o" shape, like you're blowing air through a straw, making a "whoosh" sound. Repeat the pattern three times for a total of four cycles.

If you're finding it difficult to get to the 7-second hold and 8-second exhale, you can half each number and do a 2-second inhale, 3.5-second hold, and 4-second exhale. With a little practice, you'll be able to reach 4-7-8 comfortably in no time.

You can do this breathing pattern anytime you feel stressed. Like box breathing, there have been many times I've gone to the bathroom to recenter myself and do a few rounds of 4-7-8 breathing. I've also done it sitting at my desk, out walking, or in the car. And if my mind is racing before bed, it usually quiets my thoughts and helps me drift off into dreamland.

THE PREP FRAMEWORK

Have you ever wanted to say something, but then ended up staying silent because you just didn't know how to explain it? You had a thought, but you weren't sure where to start, how much to say, or how to properly get your point across.

Knowing how to organize your thoughts and then present them in a way that's easy to understand is a significant part of being a successful communicator. You can achieve this through the PREP framework, which is designed to help you explain anything confidently and clearly. Using this framework is the most effective way to share an idea or an opinion during a meeting. Once you understand how to use it, you'll never be stuck wondering, *"How do I say this?"* ever again.

PREP stands for Point, Reason, Evidence, and Point.

Let's take a quick look at each of these.

POINT

Start by stating your point, and get right to it. In a world of busy professionals that love efficiency, now is not the time to beat around the bush. Use strong language to show that you are decisive and self-assured.

For example, your point could be, *"Communication skills are incredibly powerful."*

REASON

Next, you're going to state the reason why you believe your point. Why do you think your point is true?

Continuing with the previous example, *"Improving them will fast-track your success."*

EVIDENCE

Now, provide evidence or an example to support your reason. This could be a note from your personal experience, a statistic, a quote, or a short story. Keep this explanation short and sweet.

> *"The world's most successful business people endorse effective communication, and I've seen thousands of professionals advance their careers by developing their communication skills."*

POINT

End on a strong note by restating your original point. *"That's why communication skills are incredibly powerful."* You could also change up the wording and say, *"These skills have been proven to have a tremendous impact."*

Starting and ending with your main point is important because people tend to have the strongest recollection of the first and last things they hear. Furthermore, by restating the original point, you hammer home the key message you want them to take away.

For greater clarity on the PREP framework, here's a little summary:

- **Point**—*what* you think
- **Reason**—*why* you think it

- **Evidence**—*how* you know it to be true
- **Point**—restate *what* you think

To enhance your understanding even further, here's another example:

- **Point**—*"It's in our best interests to start outsourcing our bookkeeping."*
- **Reason**—*"It's a tedious and time-consuming job, and our time is better spent focusing on how we can grow the business."*
- **Evidence**—*"Most organizations our size use bookkeeping services because they can save time and money. In addition, these services can reduce mistakes and improve accuracy, which helps us run an organized and profitable business."*
- **Point**—*"We would be better off outsourcing our bookkeeping to a professional."*

The PREP framework can be used to explain anything, and it can be a game-changer for speaking in meetings. On top of that, it can be used in other types of verbal communication—face-to-face interactions, phone calls, video calls, and presentations. It's also beneficial for explaining yourself in written communication and can be used when writing emails, proposals, and reports.

PRACTICE AND A DIFFERENT KIND OF PREP

Practice makes progress, so you should try practicing speaking up in a less formal setting than a meeting, such as a dinner with friends or family. Even the simple act of talking when you would normally stay quiet is a great way to build the habit of using your voice.

If you're preparing for an important meeting, you could also practice speaking on your own. Just like speaking at dinner, putting in this time will make it easier to speak up in the presence of other people. Make a list of a few talking points, and then present your ideas aloud in front of the mirror. Use the PREP framework to help organize your thoughts and plan what you're going to say. You could even think of some questions people might have and work on your responses in advance.

In general, there should be some level of preparation before every meeting. Read the agenda and any materials that have been provided. If there aren't any, spend a bit of time reading about the topic on your own to make sure you're up to speed. For example, if the meeting is about choosing the best platforms to promote a product, do a quick Google search on what the experts recommend and then check out what the competition is doing.

The more you prepare and practice, the easier it will be when it's crunch time. You'll already have a good idea of what you want to say, which will help ease your mind and increase your confidence.

YOUR VOICE

The way you use your voice can have a tremendous impact on your life. A 2017 Yale study discovered that the sound of a person's voice affects how much you believe them, like them, and trust them (Kraus, 2017). You may have heard the phrase, *"It's not what you say; it's how you say it."* This is a valid statement—the tone of our voice plays an extremely important role in our verbal communication.

Imagine someone looks at you and says, *"I love you,"* but their tone sounds angry and irritated. After hearing that tone, are you going to feel warm and fuzzy and say, *"I love you too,"* or are you going to be like, *"WTF?"* Chances are, your mind will respond to their tone rather than the words they're saying.

Your tone is just as essential to effective communication as the message you're trying to get across, and it will significantly affect how people respond to you. When I was a kid, my grandmother once told me that you catch more flies with honey than vinegar. There weren't any flies around, so I was confused at the time, but now I know how much this rings true. After all, how do you feel when someone nicely asks you to do something versus barking at you?

If you want to achieve results, improve the response you get from others, and build strong relationships, it's best to focus on using a warm and friendly tone. To keep your audience's interest, it's also a good idea to use a little voice inflection to emphasize important points.

Voice inflection is when you occasionally change the pitch of your voice while speaking. When your vocal pitch is flat and monotonous, not only will you bore the people listening, but you'll also seem like you're bored yourself. Varying your pitch with voice inflection will help keep your listeners focused and engaged.

Upward voice inflection is a change in pitch from *a lower note to a higher note*. This type of inflection should be used when you're asking a question. Because raising your pitch with upward inflection has a question-sounding tone, avoid using it when making a statement. This "uptalk" can make it sound like you're unsure of what you're saying.

Downward voice inflection is a change in pitch from *a higher note to a lower note*. This type of inflection is best used at the end of a sentence. It projects confidence, power, and certainty. Lowering your pitch is the inflection you'll want to use when making a statement.

A SELF-FULFILLING PROPHECY

Do you think you're an interesting person? Because I do. I think you're interesting.

"But Ty," you say, *"You don't even know me. How can you be sure?"*

Well, I believe everyone has fascinating parts of their identities and different perspectives that I can learn from. There may be some digging beyond the surface needed to find them, but you can always come across something interesting if you look close enough.

I've always been curious about other people, but I firmly believed that no one was curious about me. It seemed like everyone thought I was boring when I spoke.

Do you know why they thought I was boring? Because *I* thought I was boring. I expected people to be uninterested in me, so I projected an attitude and energy that reflected it, which made them not listen to me. It was a self-fulfilling prophecy.

When you believe that you are dull and your ideas are bland, that's what you'll project, and that's what people will feel. It's almost like talking to a mirror, except instead of seeing your image, it's your energy and beliefs that are being reflected back to you.

If you're sitting in a chair slouching, hunched over with your arms crossed, head down, and you're speaking in a flat, monotone voice while making zero eye contact, you're not going to inspire any-body. Based on the energy you are sending out, it's clear that you don't care about what you're saying, and therefore, no one is going to listen to you or take you seriously.

So, flip the prophecy around and project the energy that you want your audience to reflect. If you hype yourself up and show interest in what you're speaking about, you will be amazed at how it changes others' perceptions of you. When I discovered this idea and started putting effort into implementing it, it was almost magical. For the first time in my life, co-workers would come up to me after meetings and say things like, *"I've never seen you speak like that," "You were actually kind of fun in there,"* or *"Thanks for keeping me awake."*

Now, as I'm giving presentations to organizations or working with individuals 1-on-1, I can immediately see the impact that my enthusiasm has on their focus and attention levels.

If you're rocking confident body language, your eyes are bright and attentive, and your voice is filled with liveliness and positivity, people will see that not only are you enjoying yourself, but you also believe your ideas are valuable and exciting. As a result, your audience will be far more engaged and interested in what you have to say, and you'll be able to capture and hold their attention more than ever before.

This is a delightful feedback loop. The more you speak with this uplifting energy, the more people will be excited to listen to you. The more people are excited to listen to you, the more excited you will be to speak. And the more excited you are to speak, the more you will speak up instead of staying silent.

THE 5 SECOND RULE

Would you consider yourself an overthinker? Have you ever got the urge to say something, started thinking about all the things that could go wrong and ended up never saying a word?

This is when Mel Robbins' *"5 Second Rule"* can be a constructive tool. When your gut tells you to speak up, you must do so within five seconds. If you pause for any longer, your fears and insecurities will rise and smother any chance of you taking action. Your overactive brain can be the main thing holding you back, so don't allow it to stop you. When you have the urge to speak, instead of stopping to think and overanalyze, do a quick countdown—5, 4, 3, 2, 1—then without hesitation, let your thoughts flow.

This is a simple but effective way to allow yourself to speak up before letting your brain censor your ideas. Make it your goal to apply this rule at least once every meeting.

THE EARLY BIRD GETS THE WORM

The earlier you speak up in the meeting, the better off you are. The longer it goes on, the more you're giving your anxiety and uncertainty the chance to grow from a small dribble into a raging storm, and the harder it will be to join the discussion.

Sometimes, we think waiting will give us more time to build courage, but instead, it usually gives us more time to think of reasons not to say anything. So, to ensure that you contribute to the meeting, make a point of talking during the first 15 minutes. It doesn't have to be a big idea; you can simply ask a question to clarify a point. The idea is that after you've opened your mouth once, you'll find it easier to do it again.

PLAY THE SIDEKICK

Many superheroes have a sidekick to help and support them. While you certainly want to be the superhero of your own story, if you're particularly timid and need a speaking up stepping stone, you can start out by playing the sidekick. If you have a close colleague who's a natural communicator, ask them to be your superhero and pull you into the discussion by asking you easy questions. Get them to ask you questions like *"Do you agree?"* or *"Do you have anything to add?"* If you're just starting out and are still working through your shyness, it's completely okay to respond with a smile and a simple *"Yes."* Everyone starts somewhere, and this can be a nice way to dip your feet into the shallow end. In time, you will become more comfortable with speaking up and ready to dive into the deep end and be the superhero of your own story. And for those of you who are already the Batman in your communication journey, keep an eye out for the Robins who could use your help.

ADD VALUE IN OTHER WAYS

To maximize your success and advance your career as fast as possible, you'll need to allow yourself to *believe* you have ideas—and that those ideas are worth sharing. That being said, if you're reading this and are insisting you have nothing to share right now, I'll offer some alternative strategies on how you can speak up for the time being.

Here are some other ways you can verbally add value to meetings:

- Asking clarifying questions
- Supporting someone else's opinion
- Steering the discussion back on track when people get off-topic

- Providing more background information on the subject
- Summarizing the main points to enhance the group's understanding

ACTION STEP

Now, it's time for action! Let's start applying what you learned. Begin by setting a goal of how many times you will speak in each meeting. If you never talk in meetings, you can start with an achievable goal of one time and choose whatever way of speaking up you find easiest.

When I started working on this many years ago as a quiet and fearful young man, the easiest thing to do was ask a question because I didn't have to think of any new ideas or spend time explaining anything.

I would ask a simple question for clarity, such as *"To confirm..."* then rephrase an important point I had just heard and make it sound like a question.

Showing support for someone else's idea is another low-key move to start with. Even throwing in a quick *"I agree"* or *"That's a great point"* is a win if you've never talked before. Small wins add up, and they give you the confidence to keep going.

Before each meeting, practice your intentional breathing techniques to relax you and optimize your state of mind. When the meeting begins, do your best to speak within the first 15 minutes, and use the 5 second rule to help with your hesitation. If you're in the early stages of your communication adventure, your main goal is first to conquer any urge you might have to stay quiet. You can even sneak in a couple of silent physiological sighs throughout the meeting for extra hits of stress relief.

As you get more comfortable, it's time to work on coming more prepared for each meeting. Plan three things you're going to say in advance—points of view, insightful questions, or new ideas—and practice what you want to say. For points that you want to make, prepare using the PREP framework. The more you think in terms of PREP, the more your brain will begin automatically organizing your thoughts in a way that allows you to communicate effectively.

Additionally, remember to think about how your audience might respond to your ideas, and practice what you'll say in return. Depending on the flow of the meeting, you may not always get to mention everything you planned for, and that's okay. Regardless of what happens, preparing in this manner will set you up to speak confidently and intelligently in every meeting.

If you've gotten to the point where you are speaking up quite often, your goal is now to increase the quality of your input rather than the quantity. Unless you're giving a presentation, you never want to be the one doing most of the talking during a meeting. Instead, you should be the person that comes prepared for each discussion, practices active listening, and contributes to the team's success by providing thoughtful points and ideas.

The next time you get the chance, try taking on a complex question that no one else wants to answer and explain your point confidently using PREP. Your strong body language and self-assured tone of voice will help reinforce your point to everyone listening. And even if you don't think you nailed the response, people will still respect you for taking one for the team in a challenging situation.

Remember that no matter where you are in your life and career, you deserve to be seen, and you deserve to be heard. You are capable of anything, you have tremendous power inside you, and you have immense value to offer. It's time to speak up, and it's time to show the world.

FREE GOODWILL

"Those who are happiest are those who do the most for others."

—*Booker T. Washington*

What's the secret to living a happier, healthier, and wealthier life? According to science, **it's the simple act of helping others.**

People who help others get to:

- Enjoy higher levels of happiness
- Make more money
- Live longer, more meaningful lives

Given these benefits, if it cost you $0, would you help someone that you don't know?

If so, I would like to ask for a favor on that person's behalf.

This person is *just like you.* They're hungry for growth, full of desire to help the world, and they know they're capable of achieving so much more. They're searching for the right information, but they don't know where to look…and that's where you come in.

The only way for our team at Advanced Growth Institute to help as many people as possible is, first, by reaching them. And while I love the quote, *"Don't judge a book by its cover,"* many people do, in fact, judge books by their covers—and their reviews.

If you have found anything you've read valuable so far, would you please take a moment right now and leave an honest review of the book? **It will cost you $0 and less than 60 seconds.**

Your review will help:

- One more awkward person feel more confident.
- One more high achiever unlock their skills.
- One more professional advance their career.
- One more person live the life of their dreams.

To help your fellow humans, all you have to do is—and it takes less than 60 seconds—leave a review.

Would you please scan the QR code below and submit a quick review before moving on? This takes you right to the review page:

I really appreciate you and your willingness to help others. If you feel good about helping someone you don't know, you are my type of person.

I like you *even more* now, and I'm extra excited to help you make incredible changes in the upcoming chapters.

Now, let's get back to building your elite communication skills.

—Your biggest fan, Ty

CHAPTER 4

LISTENING

> **"** *If we were supposed to talk more than we listen, we would have two tongues and one ear.*
>
> **—Mark Twain**

The most respected and well-liked person in a room is often not the most intelligent, the funniest, or the most charismatic. In fact, the most valued person is often the best listener. It's the person who shows genuine interest in others, asks thoughtful questions, and listens attentively.

With all of the digital distractions and information overload in modern society, many experts believe the ability to listen is going extinct. Despite the fact that we spend a large number of our waking hours listening, the majority of us aren't very good at it.

Bob Sullivan and Hugh Thompson write about this in their book *The Plateau Effect*. *"Plenty of studies examine this phenomenon. While listening is the core of most of our communications...most people stink at it. Here's one typical result. Test takers were asked to sit through a ten-minute oral presentation and, later, to describe its content. Half of adults can't do it even moments after the talk, and forty-eight hours later, 75 percent of listeners can't recall the subject matter."*

On a scale of 1–10, how would you rate your listening skills right now? Do you think others would agree?

Send a text to three key people in your life—one family member, one co-worker, and one friend—and ask them to rate your listening skills on the same scale. Did you get different answers? Did anyone close to you surprise you with a 1 or 2 out of 10? Hopefully, you received some higher ratings, but even if you got three 0s because your friends are brutally honest, don't worry. This chapter will teach you everything you need to know to turn those 0s into 10s and become a master listener.

Remember, at a fundamental level, **humans want to feel valued, appreciated, understood, and listened to.** We'll cover a wide range of techniques that do a phenomenal job of making people feel this way.

ACTIVE LISTENING AND INTENTION

Active listening means giving your complete attention to the person you're talking to. When you're actively listening, you're trying to understand the message they're conveying, absorb the presented information, and provide considerate responses. It's a skill that allows you to fully shift the focus from yourself and your own thoughts onto the person speaking to you.

Active listening includes various verbal and nonverbal skills that will help you:

- **Focus and stay engaged with the speaker**
- **Build trust and connection**
- **Maximize learning and comprehension**
- **Identify and solve problems**
- **Avoid missing out on vital information**
- **Guide the discussion to productive outcomes**

Passive listening is when you're hearing someone speak without giving them your complete attention. You're not fully engaged or putting significant effort into understanding what the speaker is saying. Many times, you're thinking about one of the thousand things rattling around in your mind as you wait for them to finish talking.

You might be thinking of what you're going to have for dinner, how your date went last night, or that there's a 50/50 chance you're living in a simulation. Regardless, what you aren't doing is paying attention to what they're saying to you.

One of the causes of poor listening is that our brains aren't applying their full power to the task. Sullivan and Thompson, who performed a study with Carnegie Mellon University on the nature of digital distractions, say that *"The human brain has the capacity to digest as much as 400 words per minute of information. But even a speaker from New York City talks at around 125 words per minute. That means three-quarters of your brain could very well be doing something else while someone is speaking to you."*

If we're only allocating a quarter of our brainpower to listening at a given moment, it's no wonder we get distracted so easily, barely remember what we heard, and leave people secretly annoyed with us after a discussion. In order to listen with your whole brain and revolutionize this ultra-powerful aspect of communication, it is extremely important to listen with **intention**.

In most cases, it's not that we're *incapable* of listening—it's that we aren't thinking about it. We're moving through the day on autopilot without considering how we want to show up in each situation. The simple act of **intention setting** changes everything. Going into every conversation with the intention of absorbing information, eliminating all distractions, and giving 100% focus will do wonders in transforming your ability to listen.

That means silencing all notifications, tuning out external noise, and being fully present with whomever you're listening to.

If you practice active listening with intention, the world will open up for you, and your life can change in astonishing ways.

Let's look at how becoming a master of active listening will benefit your career.

BUILDING TRUST AND CONNECTION

Trust is the foundation of any relationship, but it can be challenging to build. A powerful way to build trust is to actively listen when others speak to you. They'll know that when they're talking to you, they won't be interrupted, ignored, or judged. This is critical to building strong, trusting relationships in the workplace that will pay dividends throughout your career.

Actively listening also creates a safe conversational space where people feel comfortable connecting with you. This type of dynamic is particularly valuable in negotiations. If you show empathy and a genuine interest in the other party's perspectives, it will be clear that you're not just in it for selfish outcomes. They will feel that you respect them and care about their point of view, which will increase your connection, make them more open to negotiating, and ultimately help you achieve better results.

MAXIMIZING LEARNING AND COMPREHENSION

Active listening will help you understand the speaker's message, and you will absorb the information better. When you apply active listening techniques, you'll find that you can remember more details and recall them faster down the road. Since one important aspect of moving ahead in your career is expanding your knowledge, mastering active listening is critical.

IDENTIFYING AND SOLVING PROBLEMS

Active listening allows you to uncover problems more effectively, which puts you in a position to develop higher-quality solutions at an accelerated rate. You'll be asking strategic questions to help you uncover more data, and the more data you have, the more efficiently you will discover, define, and solve problems. This skill alone will make you a valuable member of any team.

PREVENTING VITAL INFORMATION FROM BEING MISSED

When you actively listen to someone else, you focus deeply on their message. Since you're paying close attention, you are far less likely to miss any key information they might convey. Whenever you're learning something new, receiving instructions, or getting a message you need to pass along, it's imperative that you don't miss anything significant.

Now, let's move on to more skills you can apply to become an active listener. Make sure to practice these techniques frequently so that they become embedded in your brain and part of your everyday life.

PARAPHRASING

Repetition is a fundamental part of learning, and it's also an important part of active listening—in this case, verbally. Restating what the speaker said confirms you heard them correctly and that you're on the same page. It also shows them that you're paying attention, which is becoming increasingly uncommon in today's world.

You don't have to turn into a recorder and replay exactly what you hear, of course. It's better to **rephrase what was said in your words—also known as paraphrasing**—because it sounds more natural and shows you understood the essence of their message.

This technique forces you to understand the other person's point of view before rushing in to present your side of the story. When you paraphrase what someone has said, you're taking the time to grasp their message instead of instantly jumping to your next thought.

For example, your manager might say, *"We're not moving forward with your idea because the costs ended up being higher than expected, and we don't believe those costs are justified."*

Instead of getting on your high horse and immediately coming up with a rebuttal, paraphrase what he said. *"It sounds like your main concern is that it's going to cost more than we initially thought, and you don't see enough value to spend the money."*

By taking this approach, you show your manager that you heard what they said and you're paying attention. It also stops you in your tracks and helps you understand the opposing viewpoint. If you hadn't taken the time to paraphrase what they said, you'd be more likely to have a short-sighted emotional reaction. For example, your first response may be to get defensive and say, *"But the costs are justified. I already explained this to you."*

Instead, you're giving yourself a few moments to consider what they're saying and respond in a way that doesn't lead to a combative discussion. Now, you can ask for more time to improve your idea, which will lead to results rather than pointless arguments.

Paraphrasing is an effective way of validating what someone else is saying. It's also a great tool for building strong relationships because people love to see that their message is being heard. And because active listening is becoming so rare, when you become one of the few people that do this well in your organization, you will become even more valued.

Here are some more examples of paraphrasing:

- *It sounds like you need more information before moving forward.*
- *If I understand correctly, it sounds like your biggest challenge right now is generating quality leads.*
- *It sounds like we need to shift our focus more to our sales funnels instead of our website.*
- *It sounds like you're hesitant about looping in the operations team because of how they handled the last project.*

Did you notice how each statement includes **"it sounds like"**? I learned this from Chris Voss, author of *Never Split the Difference: Negotiating As If Your Life Depended On It*. Many communication resources teach you to begin paraphrasing with "what I'm hearing is," which isn't as effective because it contains the word "I." The word "I" tends to put people's guard up because it suggests you're more interested in yourself than the person speaking.

"It sounds like" is always received better, and it also protects you if your paraphrased statement is incorrect. Because you're not explicitly saying "you said this," you're simply saying "it sounds like this," it decreases the risk of the person getting offended and enhances their receptivity throughout the interaction.

OPEN-ENDED QUESTIONS

Asking open-ended questions is a great way to inspire productive dialogue. It encourages your conversation partner to expand on their thoughts and reveal more information.

Open-ended questions are questions that begin with "how" or "what" and unlike closed-ended questions, they cannot be answered with a simple "yes" or "no." The nature of the open-ended question makes the person reply with a more detailed response.

For example, asking someone, *"Do you want to lead this project?"* is a closed-ended question because it can be answered with a one-word answer, "yes" or "no." Asking *"What do you think about leading this project?"* makes them explain their thoughts and give more information.

Asking open-ended questions that start with "how" or "what" gives the other person the spotlight to share their thoughts—making them feel as if they are in control—even though you're the one asking questions.

You'd be surprised by how much people will reveal when you get them talking in this way. Asking these types of questions can get you valuable information about anything you want to know more about—people, organizations, challenges, opportunities, etc.

Here are some examples of open-ended questions you should be using regularly:

- *How would you like to proceed?*
- *What are our next steps?*
- *What is preventing us from moving forward?*
- *What's the biggest challenge you face?*
- *How can I help you?*
- *What are you looking to accomplish with this project?*
- *What about this is most important to you?*
- *How can I help make this better for us?*
- *What bothered you most about their response?*
- *How would you like to solve this problem?*
- *What do you have in mind?*
- *What changes would you like to see?*

- *If this meeting, project, partnership, etc. achieved everything you could hope for, what would that look like?*

ACKNOWLEDGING EMOTIONS

If the person you're speaking with is emotional, you aren't going to get much accomplished if you ignore their emotions and just keep talking. A wide range of emotions is to be expected from both genders—don't think that just because you're in a professional setting, people will magically set aside their feelings and be completely rational all the time.

Humans are way more complex than that. Studies show that we rely more on emotion and less on rational thought when making decisions than we like to believe. Gerald Zaltman, a Harvard professor, explains in his book *How Customers Think: Essential Insights into the Mind of the Market* that consumers rely far more on emotion than logic when making purchasing decisions (Zaltman, 2003). Furthermore, research has shown that people with damage to the areas of the brain responsible for emotion, such as the amygdala, are deficient when it comes to decision-making (Gupta et al., 2011).

No matter the situation you're in, you can't expect emotions not to be involved. And when you're with someone who is stressed out and in a poor place emotionally, they often can't see past their feelings, which will result in poor decision-making and could even lead to conflict.

If you acknowledge their emotions, you're giving them precisely what they need, which is to feel heard and respected. You don't necessarily have to agree with what they're feeling; you just have to do your best to understand and acknowledge them in the right way.

Here are some examples:

- *You seem frustrated with these time delays.*
- *You sounded a bit angry after that meeting. How is everything?*
- *It sounds like you're upset about something. What can I do to help?*
- *It seems like you're a bit on edge the last few days. How are you doing?*

Notice that we're gently labeling what we believe the speaker is feeling without coming across as aggressive—note the "it sounds like" with some added "it seems like" statements. We can also add an open-ended question to encourage more information. This gives them the opportunity to confirm or deny our label and provide more insight into what they're thinking and feeling.

Understanding what someone is feeling is key to effective communication. After all, the person may seem angry, but they could just be a bit annoyed. You're going to handle the person a lot differently depending on what they're feeling, so it's important to give them the chance to explain.

NONVERBAL TECHNIQUES

Incorporating nonverbal communication is another meaningful part of becoming a master listener. Let's take a quick look at the nonverbal techniques you should be using to show you're fully engaged with your conversation partner.

NODDING YOUR HEAD

Nodding is often a signifier of agreement, and it can also symbolize comprehension and empathy. When you're nodding while someone else is talking, they feel as if you are hearing and understanding them.

Essentially, your head nods are saying, *"I understand you. Please continue."*

Just like smiling, you should keep it subtle. Nodding too enthusiastically will look bizarre and distract the speaker, and nodding too quickly can make you look impatient.

Bobbleheads should only be used as fun novelty gifts—not as inspiration for elite communication. Instead, practice slow, gentle nods. Three in a row is the sweet spot. These are the best nods for encouraging a productive discussion.

MAINTAINING EYE CONTACT

Maintaining eye contact with the person speaking is another indicator that you are actively listening. It's also harder for your mind to wander when making consistent eye contact, which helps you pay closer attention to their message. As you learned in Chapter 2, it's best to make eye contact around 60-70% of the time.

OPEN BODY LANGUAGE

Next, make sure you're maintaining open body language. Also covered in Chapter 2, open body language means sitting (or standing) straight with arms and legs uncrossed, shoulders back, and head up.

I recommend keeping a special eye on what your arms and hands are doing. They can develop a mind of their own, and if you aren't careful, you might end up crossing your arms without realizing it. This will hurt your communication because it's a closed position that can suggest you're trying to "block out" what you're hearing. You might cross your arms because it feels comfortable, but it sends negative messages to the speaker when you're listening. It signals a person who is distant, defensive, or insecure.

Remember to keep those hands visible. When standing, keep your arms by your sides or steeple your hands. While you're sitting, rest your arms on the table in front of you or on the arms of your chair. It's also a good idea to lean in a bit towards the person talking, as it shows a high level of attentiveness.

Finally, I recommend **fronting**, which means pointing your whole body toward the person speaking—everything from your head to your toes. Positioning your body this way is a sign of respect and shows the other person that you are completely focused on them.

AVOID FIDGETING

Fidgeting can indicate boredom or nervousness. If you're fidgeting, it looks like you aren't interested in what someone is saying, which can be frustrating for them and negatively affect your relationship. Remember, you can use the hand steeple so your hands have a position to hold. Additionally, you can take notes on what the person is saying if it's appropriate. It'll keep your hands busy, and there's the added benefit of having a record of the critical points that were discussed.

SMILING

Smiling is a surprisingly useful technique when you're listening to another person. It makes the speaker feel like you care about what they're saying while inspiring a feeling of understanding and intimacy.

Of course, that doesn't mean you should grin like a maniac, especially if the topic isn't anything to smile about. The last person you want to be channeling is The Joker. You don't want anyone inching for their phone to call the cops because you're giving off supervillain-in-hiding vibes.

In the case of a highly serious topic where smiling would make you seem insensitive, just raise the corners of your mouth slightly. Think of it a bit like the Mona Lisa smile. That slight upturn of your lips won't make you look happy about the speaker having a problem, but it will prevent you from looking angry or annoyed.

ACTION STEP

Now, it's time to take all the active listening techniques and put them to good use. Here's a summary for you to follow:

- Set an intention to actively listen before every interaction
- Eliminate all distractions and tune out external noise
- Give your complete attention to the person speaking
- Focus closely on understanding and absorbing their message
- Paraphrase their words back to them
- Ask open-ended "how" or "what" questions
- Acknowledge their emotions
- Nod your head slowly
- Maintain eye contact 60-70% of the time
- Keep your body language upright and open
- Lean in slightly to demonstrate interest
- Keep your hands visible

- Face your entire body towards the speaker—also known as fronting
- Avoid fidgeting
- Smile (the seriousness of the topic will determine your level of smile)

By using these techniques when listening, you will be in the best position to **maximize your learning, comprehension, and problem solving abilities.**

In addition, you will make others feel **heard, understood, valued, and respected.** When you apply active listening, you can make a person feel like the center of your world at that moment, which is a **powerful way to gain influence.**

Like all communication skills we're learning, these active listening skills can and should be used in any setting, not just in your professional life. Using these techniques throughout your workday *and* during your personal interactions will have you improving at Usain Bolt level speeds.

CHAPTER 5

READING NONVERBAL CUES

" *What you do speaks so loudly that I cannot hear what you say."*

—Ralph Waldo Emerson

N ow that you know how to optimize your own body language for maximum success, it's time to start focusing on other people's bodies. I mean that in the most respectful, communication-focused way possible. **Reading the nonverbal cues of others is a powerful skill that gives you access to an epic amount of unspoken information. It offers tremendous insight into what a person is thinking and feeling—without them having to say a word.**

Nonverbal cues are always more trustworthy than words because people don't have as much conscious control over them. A lot of our body language is based on emotions, which means these cues happen automatically instead of intentionally. If there's a discrepancy between the words you're hearing and the nonverbal cues you're seeing, you're better off trusting the messages you receive from the nonverbal. Having the key to unlock this type of knowledge puts you at an enormous advantage in every situation.

LORD OF THE EYES

You've probably heard some version of the quote, *"The eyes are the windows to the soul."* Cheesy as it is, there is some accuracy to it on a practical level. Our eyes are very expressive and can give away our real feelings without us even realizing it's happening.

That's why, when communicating with someone, you want to pay very close attention to their eyes. If they aren't making direct eye contact, odds are they're either nervous or are disinterested in the conversation. Looking down, in particular, is an indicator of passiveness and anxiety.

Glancing at a particular place or person can be a sign of what somebody wants. For example, if they keep sneaking in peaks at the door, they're likely waiting for someone to arrive, or they're looking to make an exit. If they're straight up staring at the door and ignoring the person talking, they'd likely leave scorch marks on the floor if they were given the opportunity to leave. And when the person you're speaking with keeps glancing over at someone else, it's a good indicator that they want to talk to them.

There was once a theory that said you could tell when a person was lying by watching the direction of their eyes. The idea was that if a right-handed person looked to the right, they were using the right side of their brain—the creative half—which meant they were constructing a lie. On the other hand, eyes looking to the left meant activity in the left side of the brain—the rational half—indicating the person was telling the truth. This theory used to be so widely accepted that it was used to train police and military interrogators. The idea was debunked in 2012 when a study conducted by a team of researchers in Canada and the UK proved it was nothing but a myth (Wiseman et al., 2012).

If someone is rubbing their eyelids, they are likely stressed. This is particularly true if you ask them a difficult question. By rubbing their eyelids, they're disrupting eye contact and self-soothing, which helps reduce anxiety and stress levels.

Another thing to look for when it comes to the eyes is how a person is blinking. It might sound a little strange, but how quickly a person blinks can tell you a lot about how they're feeling.

Humans tend to blink faster when deep in thought or stressed. **They might also be blinking quicker than usual if they're _lying_ to you.** Increased blink rate can be an indicator of deception, but it's not a guarantee on its own. This is a cue for you to keep watching them closely.

Further evidence of the deception would be touching their face, particularly their nose. Researchers found using thermographic cameras that when people tell a lie, their nose actually heats up! This rise in temperature can make the nerves in your nose feel a little tingly, creating the urge to touch or scratch it when lying. The nose of a liar may not grow like Pinocchio's, but it might get *itchy*.

MOUTH TRAP

Our mouths are essential tools. And this is coming from someone who puts tape over his mouth before bed to ensure nasal breathing during sleep. That's right—between talking, eating, and other pleasurable activities (wink wink), our mouths play a huge role in our lives.

Think about a smile. It's a simple but powerful gesture that can have a massive impact on people. There are all sorts of smiles, but you'll want to specifically watch for the difference between genuine and fake smiles.

When someone smiles genuinely, their whole face will be engaged, particularly the eyes and the area around them. Real smiles cause the eyes to light up a bit, and the muscles around the eyes will contract.

Conversely, when someone gives you a fake smile, only the muscles around the mouth engage. If it's hard for you to imagine, head over to your nearest mirror. Think about a person that annoys you, and then smile. Now, look at your face and see which areas are engaged. Chances are, only your mouth moved, and the rest of your face stayed the same.

Now, take a moment to think of someone or something that makes you happy. I *highly* recommend Googling "dogs with sunglasses." Smile again. What does it look like this time? If it's authentic—and it should be after seeing those cool canines—you'll notice a difference in your eyes, and the muscles around your eyes will have contracted. That's the easiest way to spot the difference between a genuine and fake smile.

Naturally, a genuine smile indicates that the person you're talking to is enjoying themselves, while a fake smile is meant to hide real emotions. This face will fool some people, but not you. You'll be able to tell that their face is misaligned with the emotions they're trying to project.

The mouth can be more revealing than any other part of the face. Humans exhibit tiny expressions with their mouths, called micro-expressions, that last less than a second. These are so quick and instinctual that most people have no idea they ever cross their faces. It's almost impossible to hide these half-second micro-expressions.

For example, there could be a **contempt** micro-expression before a smile that happens so quickly, you'd never notice unless you were a communication enthusiast intentionally watching for cues. The contempt micro-expression is when only one side of the mouth gets raised. Think of a smug-looking smirk. This is a sign of dislike, disrespect, or disapproval.

Dr. John Gottman, marriage counselor and relationship researcher, found that these contempt cues were a surprisingly accurate predictor of divorce. If one or both partners showed contempt for their spouse during his initial interview, there was a *93% chance* the couple would end up getting divorced.

There's also the **disgust** micro-expression, which is a sudden raise of the upper lip and crinkle of the nose. And if the eyebrows raise, eyes widen, and the mouth opens vertically like an O, you've just witnessed the micro-expression for **surprise**.

The **fear** micro-expression is similar to surprise, but the mouth will open horizontally instead of vertically.

Another thing to watch out for is **pursed lips**—sucking the lips in or pulling them inward into a hard line. We purse our lips when we're trying to avoid saying something, which means we are either annoyed about not having the opportunity to speak or not comfortable stating what's on our mind. You'll often see this expression when a person wants to say something but knows that they shouldn't.

This is another cue that a person is **lying**; it's like they're trying to keep their mouth tightly shut to prevent themselves from saying anything incriminating. If you watch past interviews of Lance Armstrong, you'll often see lip purses when he's lying about using performance-enhancing drugs.

What do you do if you see these cues in your professional life? Let's look at an example. If a client agrees to your next steps, and you see a fake smile or pursed lips, there's a chance they aren't sold on moving forward. It's interesting how some people will choose to agree to something to avoid confrontation, only to back out afterward when it's easier. If you're reading nonverbal cues, instead of wondering, *"What did I do wrong?"* after the deal falls through, you get the opportunity to address their concerns in the moment.

If you spot a nonverbal cue that indicates uncertainty or mismatched emotions, it's time to dig deeper with open-ended questions. In this situation, you would ask a question like, *"What are your thoughts on moving forward?"* or *"How confident are you in these next steps?"* or *"What can we do to make sure these next steps happen smoothly?"*

Each time you ask an open-ended question, it forces the person to elaborate on their thoughts, making it increasingly difficult for them to keep half-heartedly agreeing without explaining what they really think.

FOOT FOR THOUGHT

Our feet were made for more than walking—they also tell a lot about our intentions during a conversation. The majority of people don't think about body language, but advanced communicators will do their best to control their eye contact, hands, and the position of their upper bodies. That being said, very few ever think about feet.

Similar to sneaking glances at a particular person or place, people will also subconsciously point their feet to where they want to go. This is true whether they're standing or sitting, and it's a great way to sneakily know how people feel about each other in a group setting.

If two people are talking and one of them has their feet pointed noticeably in another direction or towards the door, it's evident that they'd prefer to be elsewhere. If their feet are pointed directly at someone else, there's a strong chance they'd rather be speaking to that person. You can gain fascinating insight with this awareness, so start keeping an eye out for those feet (just be discreet about it.)

A HEAD GIVEAWAY

You can learn even more about a person's communication by observing their head. The way they move their noggin can indicate their interest in the conversation as well as their current level of patience. If they nod slowly, it's a good indicator that they care about what you're saying and want you to keep going.

On the other hand, nodding quickly can indicate that the person is becoming impatient and has heard enough. At this point, they're hoping you will stop talking so they can jump in and say their piece.

If someone is tilting their head to the side while you're talking, it shows that they're interested in what you're saying. On the other hand, if someone is tilting their head back, it can imply a level of suspicion or uncertainty.

Like the direction of eyes and feet, the direction a person orients their head can also indicate who or what they are interested in. People tend to point their head or face towards people they have an affinity for. If you're in a meeting with a new group and trying to figure out the dynamic, you can often tell the most powerful person in the room based on how frequently everyone else turns their head to look at them.

Finally, our foreheads are involved in the classic **shame** cue. When someone feels shame, they lightly touch their forehead with their fingers and break eye contact with everyone, usually looking downward. If you see the shame cue, it means the person feels embarrassed or uncomfortable about something that happened or something that was said. If you want to keep your rapport with this person, make sure not to shame their shame! Offer them support and acceptance. You could even share something vulnerable yourself to show empathy and help them feel better.

LINT PICKING

An incredibly subtle nonverbal cue to watch for is lint picking, which is when people touch their knees or thighs as if they're brushing away crumbs. This negative, reflexive gesture symbolizes getting rid of something they don't want or view as annoying. When someone is lint picking, it's likely a sign that they're dismissing what you're trying to say.

You might notice someone doing this after you've introduced a benefit that they don't see value in. It could also occur during a negotiation if you're presenting evidence that they don't believe. Essentially, it's a subconscious sign of dismissal or disagreement, so when you see it, it's best not to barrel forward in your presentation. Instead, it's time to expand on your point and ask open-ended questions to gain more information about the lint picker's perspective.

CONFRONTATION CUES

It would be difficult to avoid conflict at work altogether, especially when dealing with tight deadlines, massive projects, or strong personalities. However, if you watch for certain cues, you will be more prepared to deal with the situation effectively, which means de-escalating it before emotions get out of hand.

Aggressively sticking the chin up and out (also known as jutting) or planting hands on the hips with feet spread widely apart (adopting a battle stance) are two cues that a person is angry.

Jutting your chin is the equivalent of saying, *"Come at me. I'm not scared of you."*

Professional fighters know this well. The best way to knock a person out is to land a hit on the chin or jaw area—and the point of the chin, in particular, is the most vulnerable to a gnarly knockout blow. Opening up and sticking out the chin is a cocky move that says you don't see the other fighter as a threat. Outside of the ring, jutting the chin is an instinctual response that can happen in any confrontation, and it's a dead giveaway of a person's anger.

The wide-legged battle stance with hands forcefully on hips is meant to take up space and is a very territorial move. People may automatically adopt the battle stance when upset in an attempt to show that they are superior.

When you see these confrontation cues, your next move will depend on the person's level of anger. If it seems manageable, you can work on calming them down by giving them the opportunity to feel heard and understood. This is when you'd use your active listening skills—acknowledging their emotions, paraphrasing, and using open-ended questions. For example, *"It seems like you're irritated. What can be done to help?"* Sometimes, all a person wants in that moment is to feel like others care about them and their emotions.

That being said, if they're flying off the handle, it's best to say, *"It looks like we're better off revisiting this another time,"* and quickly exit stage left.

THAT'S ENOUGH FOR TODAY

Remember in high school when the bell was about to ring, and two minutes before class ended, you'd start packing away your things? You wanted to be ready to hightail it out of there the second that bell rang. Some of us still do this now at our jobs, but we try to be sneakier about it, and we don't have a bell to guarantee our departure time.

Keep an eye out for this type of behavior. Suppose you're giving a presentation or running a meeting, and the decision-maker starts slowly putting away their things. In that case, it's best to skip over anything that isn't imperative and reach a conclusion as soon as possible.

People also tend to do certain things with their bodies when they're ready to leave, like lightly slapping their thighs, tapping their shoes on the floor, or drumming on the desk with their knuckles or palms. If they're really getting antsy, they'll put their hands on their knees and shift their upper body forward as if they're getting ready to stand. When you see these types of actions from the key people you're trying to influence, it's time to put the pedal to the metal. If you're only seeing these cues from your sloth-like co-worker who leaves at 4:58 p.m. every day, keep doing your thing.

As you begin observing the nonverbal cues of others, you may be surprised by what you find. People are constantly sending messages about what they think and feel, and they're doing so without even realizing it. When you learn to read and interpret these nonverbal cues, you'll have access to a whole new world of insight into the people around you. Remember, a significant part of listening is hearing what *isn't* being said aloud.

NONVERBAL MIRRORING

Research shows that we are naturally drawn to people that are similar to us. When we believe someone is like us, we're more likely to build a connection, trust them, like them, and listen to them. To gain the benefits of perceived similarity with anyone you want to influence, you can use a communication tactic called mirroring.

Nonverbal mirroring is when you match the other person's body position, posture, and gestures to help create powerful connections.

This type of mirroring happens all the time, but it's usually done subconsciously and happens when someone feels a strong bond with the person they're speaking to. With a little awareness and effort, you can use mirroring consciously to have more success in every conversation.

Many high-level professionals use mirroring to increase the level of connection during their interactions, which allows them to build and strengthen their relationships at work at a much faster rate. It's been proven to be an excellent rapport builder that helps your bosses, co-workers, and clients like and trust you more during conversations.

"Does it actually work?"

Whether it's a 1-on-1 coaching client or a boardroom full of executives, I've heard this question from clients on numerous occasions. I can appreciate a healthy level of skepticism, so let's dive into some research and look at four studies that illustrate the power of mirroring.

Journalist Benedict Carey wrote an article called *"You Remind Me of Me"* in the New York Times covering various experiments that proved mirroring works. In one study, researchers showed participants a series of advertisements and asked for their opinion. While they were looking at the advertisements, the researcher mirrored the posture and position of half the participants, including the positioning of their legs and arms. Later, the researcher pretended to drop some pens on the floor accidentally. The participants that the researcher had mirrored throughout the experiment proved to be *2–3 times more likely* to pick up the pens than those who hadn't been mirrored.

A Duke University study supported these findings. In this particular experiment, students tried a new sports drink and then answered a number of questions. The person conducting the interview mirrored the posture and movements of half of the students. The mirroring was done with a delay of one to two seconds to ensure the participants didn't catch on to what was happening. When the interview was finished, the participants who had been mirrored were far more likely to try the drink than those who hadn't. They were also more likely to state that they'd buy it, and more of them felt that the drink would succeed if launched to market.

In an article entitled *"Use Mirroring to Connect with Others,"* published in the Wall Street Journal, Sue Shellenbarger covered experiments dealing with mirroring. A 2011 experiment in France was performed with retail salespeople and 129 customers. The salespeople were instructed to mimic their customers' nonverbal and verbal cues. Some salespeople followed these instructions, and some didn't mirror and worked as per usual. At the end of the experiment, the employees that did mirror their customers sold considerably more products than the ones who didn't. And that wasn't the only benefit. The customers who had been mirrored walked away with a better opinion of the store than those who hadn't been mirrored, proving how important human connection is to purchasing decisions and overall perception (Shellenbarger, 2016).

Another study published in 2008 in the Journal of Experimental Social Psychology involved 62 students required to negotiate with one another. The students who took the time to mirror their negotiating partners' posture and verbal communication style were successful 67% of the time in the negotiation. Conversely, those who didn't engage in mirroring only managed to reach a consensus 12.5% of the time.

Between these four studies, mirroring was shown to make others more likely to:

- **Help and support us**
- **Listen to our suggestions and believe in our success**
- **Buy from us and view us favorably**
- **Cooperate with us in a negotiation**

Fortunately, mirroring is a skill anyone can learn, just like everything else in this book. If you ever want to see an expert at work when it comes to mirroring, study politicians when they're talking. Politicians go through extensive training on mirroring in order to build as many connections as possible. Without these connection-building skills, they would have no chance of success. After all, politics is all about winning people over, and that's very difficult to do if you can't build a connection with someone.

ACTION STEP

Start by being more mindful of the mirroring that happens in your daily life. Because mirroring is typically a subconscious byproduct of connection, it's already happening around you in some way. Watch for things like similar body positions and hand gestures in your interactions and when observing others. Two people taking a drink at the same time is even a form of mirroring, and it's a common one in restaurant settings.

As you build your awareness, you can start incorporating it yourself. Begin with mirroring body position and posture. For example, if you and your conversation partner are standing in a hallway talking, allow the position of your body to align with theirs. When this becomes more habitual, you can add hand gestures and any other movements you observe.

When you're already armed with knowledge on nonverbal communication, adding in mirroring makes it even easier to recognize what the person's body is telling you about their thoughts and feelings. The key to optimal relationship-building goes beyond mimicking a person's actions—it's also about becoming attuned to their feelings and exhibiting empathy. That's the most powerful way to create a connection and build influence.

Keep in mind, it's best to be cautious when mirroring nonverbal communication. If you replicate someone's gestures or a change in their body position, don't do it at the exact same moment. Instead, wait a couple of seconds and then do something similar. If you mirror them too frequently and do it at the same time with the same movement, they may catch on. If you're too obvious, they may think you're mocking them, and that's the opposite of what you want.

Furthermore, you don't have to put pressure on yourself to mirror everything a person does. For example, suppose you pick up on a negative nonverbal cue, like pursed lips. If it's a negative cue, it's better to take note of it, consider what may have caused it, and keep your body language positive rather than mirror their negativity.

Once you're aware of the negative cue, you have a few strategic options. The first option is the open-ended question. As you may be realizing, this is one of our go-to communication moves for any interaction. Why? Because it's extremely effective at uncovering crucial information while simultaneously showing that we care about the other person and value what they have to say.

So, instead of ignoring the nonverbal cue every time, use an open-ended question, such as, *"How do you feel about that?"* or *"What are your thoughts?"* Rather than asking, *"Is everything okay?"* or *"Are you alright?"* which can be easily brushed off with a quick *"yes"* or *"no,"* these questions work wonders at getting people to tell the truth and explain what they're thinking. You're also giving them the opportunity to express themselves, which is an incredibly likable thing to do.

The second option is to demonstrate concern, but the key is to be indirect. If you're too direct with your language, they'll feel put on the spot. Remember, if they haven't said anything and it's all coming through in their body language, they might be hesitant to reveal their emotions. You'll get a much better response if you're indirect and gentle about it.

Using what we learned about acknowledging emotions last chapter, you would say, *"It seems like you're a little uncomfortable with this,"* or *"It seems like you're a little hesitant,"* or *"It seems like there's a bit of resistance."* Notice that because we're responding to something we saw, not something we heard, we're using *"it seems like"* to begin our statements instead of *"it sounds like."*

You'll find that when you take a moment to explore a negative nonverbal cue, the cause is often surprisingly easy to resolve. It might stem from something that they're unsure of or hesitant about, and all they needed was a little reassurance from you. You may have forgotten to respond to an email that they needed, and they can't focus on what you're saying right now because they still need that info. When you uncover this, you can apologize and respond right away.

There are even times when you'll learn that their negative cue had nothing to do with you and was caused by something else that's bothering them. In this case, not only is it valuable to know your relationship with them hasn't been compromised, but you're also now in a position to offer a supportive pair of active listening ears.

Before going too deep on reading nonverbal cues, make sure you've spent enough time working on your active listening skills. Focusing on one skill at a time is a more effective way of learning than trying to figure out ten different things at once. Once you're confident in your active listening skills and are noticing considerable improvements in your interactions, move on to reading nonverbal cues.

Remember, nonverbal cues provide the most valuable insight when observed throughout the course of an entire conversation. Seeing a single cue one time doesn't mean you know someone's thoughts or feelings with 100% certainty. The key here is to look for repeated cues and patterns. As you progress, add mirroring those nonverbal cues to your communication repertoire.

When you get comfortable with all of the techniques from this chapter, every interaction you have will change. You'll have access to a whole new world of unspoken information and relationship building, and you will be at a tremendous advantage in every situation.

CHAPTER 6

MORE ORAL

" *Good communication is as stimulating as black coffee, and just as hard to sleep after."*

—Anne Morrow Lindbergh

You've learned to walk the walk, now let's keep learning how to talk the talk. Let's jump into more oral communication strategies.

VERBAL MIRRORING

In the previous chapter, you learned that nonverbal mirroring is an excellent rapport builder and a powerful way to make your bosses, co-workers, and clients like and trust you more during conversations. You learned about matching your conversation partner's body position, posture, and gestures. Now, we'll take mirroring a step further and explore the impact of *verbal* mirroring.

Verbal mirroring is when you speak in a way that closely matches your conversation partner's vocal tone, volume, and speed. People feel drawn to voices similar to theirs, which makes mirroring useful to increase engagement.

Many top professionals use both verbal and nonverbal mirroring to rapidly increase the level of connection during their interactions, allowing them to build stronger relationships and gain influence quickly.

Now, the idea isn't to obsess over copying a person's voice. You want to model their communication style while maintaining your individuality and authenticity. Mirroring doesn't have to be extreme to the point of sounding unnatural.

While you don't have to worry about flawlessly matching the other person's speed and volume, you do want to become more aligned with the way they're speaking. For example, if your colleague is talking calmly and quietly, and you sound like you're in the club after your fourth Jager Bomb, they will sense the disconnect and feel uncomfortable. Simply slowing down your speech and lowering your voice will help you build a connection.

Likewise, if you're talking with your Vice President first thing in the morning, and it seems like they just excitedly pounded three cups of coffee, it's probably not the time for long, dramatic pauses. Instead, do your best to match their energy, tone, speed, and volume. Again, don't worry about pushing yourself too hard to the point of sounding unnatural. We all have a range of speeds, volumes, and tones that feel comfortable to us, and the more you practice varying these parts of your voice when mirroring, the wider your range will grow.

Right now, your goal is to simply narrow the vocal gap between you and the person you're speaking with as much as possible, which will go a long way in helping you build rapport with everyone. When you have better relationships with everyone in your professional life, your workdays become easier and more enjoyable, you get more respect from others, and you'll be in a position for your career to advance at an elevated rate.

ACTION STEP

The first step to improving your voice is to learn how you sound right now. Use a voice recorder app on your cell phone to record yourself in different work situations and see how your voice changes. Awareness is crucial—once you're aware of how different situations affect your voice, you can work on the specific areas that need improvement.

You may notice that your voice sounds natural and smooth when talking to your favorite co-worker, but when you speak to a particular executive, your voice tends to get quieter in a way that makes you sound less confident. Most of the time, we have no idea we are doing things that put us at a disadvantage until we take the time to analyze ourselves. Now, the next time that executive speaks to you, you know to focus on maintaining your usual volume and keeping your voice strong.

Once you start making mirroring a regular practice, use these recordings to see how natural your voice sounds while mirroring others. This is a great way to track your progress as your skills improve each week.

PHONE CALLS

Ah, phone calls. When the telephone was invented in 1876, the way humans communicated soared to a whole new level. Today, the ability to make successful calls is an essential skill if you want to advance your career as fast as possible. Phone calls play a significant role in our professional lives—they're much faster than meeting someone face-to-face and more personal than sending an email.

Some people are complete naturals on the phone. The phone rings, and they transform into Leonardo DiCaprio in the Wolf of Wall Street when he's hammering out sales in the early scenes. Others aren't quite as gifted, and some of us are utterly terrified at the thought of using the phone.

One time, I sat in a cubicle and stared at my phone for two hours before dialing any numbers. I just sat there...staring and contemplating my existence. When I finally mustered up the courage to start dialing, I remember pressing three numbers—3, 0, 6—and then I gave up. I made the switch from staring at the phone to staring at the wall until it was time to go home for the day.

Regardless of where you're at right now, if you follow the tips in this chapter, you'll find that every call becomes easier and more enjoyable. You'll feel more comfortable and confident, and you'll ultimately get better results on all of your calls. What you're about to learn helped me go from an awkward phone starer to someone who confidently speaks to CEOs and closes high-ticket sales over the phone.

PREPARATION

Preparing the right way before making a phone call will ease your mind and automatically make you sound more confident. If you have several points to discuss and you want to make sure you hit all of them, make a quick bulleted list as an outline for your call. Keep the points as concise as possible—their only purpose is to jog your memory and keep you on track.

Now, establish the goal of the call. Is it gathering or giving information, making arrangements, introducing your product/service, getting feedback, obtaining approval, or something else? It will be much easier for you to stay focused if you go in with a clear purpose. This makes for a more efficient and effective conversation, which your conversation partner will appreciate. We're all busy, so the last thing you want is to make the person on the other line think you're unorganized or that you don't respect their time.

PULL UP A PIC

Have you ever talked to someone and felt really connected? Almost as if you've known them for years? If you thought I was going to start talking about past lives, that was another part of the book that didn't make the cut. Something about having "nothing to do with communication skills." Another comment from the editor that was initially hurtful but relatively accurate.

So, what's a more relevant reason for this connection? It's a biological response that is the result of oxytocin. Oxytocin is a hormone associated with trust, empathy, and relationship-building, and it's often referred to as the cuddle hormone or love drug. The body releases this hormone when we're with someone we feel connected to.

We produce oxytocin in various ways, including physical touch and eye contact. Neither of those is possible over the phone, making it challenging to achieve the same level of connection on a call.

One way to replicate this is to pull up a picture of the person you're talking to while on the phone with them. That way, it no longer feels as if you're talking to an invisible robot. It cements the fact that the voice on the other end is, in fact, a real person.

So, if you want to maximize your chances of a positive interaction, open a picture from one of their social media profiles before the call. It will help you feel more connected, and this will create a warmer tone of voice. People will feel that warmth right away, which will help strengthen your relationship and make the call more successful.

OPTIMIZE YOUR STATE OF MIND

One of the most powerful ways to change the outcome of your phone calls is to optimize your state of mind before dialing. **Being in the right state of mind will influence your tone of voice, the energy you give off, and how the person on the other line perceives you.**

When your state of mind is genuinely positive, energetic, and upbeat, you'll find people are far more receptive to what you have to say. It becomes easier to build rapport with them, and they're significantly more likely to respond favorably to your requests.

This ultimately leads to more success, a more positive interaction for both parties, and more enjoyment for you during your workday.

So, how do you change your state of mind? It's a simple five-step process that takes about 20 seconds in total. **Sit up straight, breathe, visualize, smile, then dial.**

Sit Up Straight

Remember, body language has a direct influence on your state of mind. Begin with confident body language by sitting up straight, pulling your shoulders down and back, and holding your head up high. This will give you a boost of energy and confidence, which will naturally project into your voice and enhance how you sound over the phone.

Breathe

Next, take two physiological sighs. As you learned in Chapter 3, the physiological sigh is two consecutive inhales through the nose (one long, one short) followed by one long exhale through the mouth. The duration of your exhale should be longer than your two inhales. Breathing this way has been proven to increase relaxation, reduce stress, and improve mental clarity.

Visualize

As you take your breaths, close your eyes and imagine something or someone that makes you happy. It could be a loved one, a pet, or a favorite place. It could even be an object or an event—anything that brings you joy.

If you're having trouble actually "seeing" anything in your mind, simply thinking of it works just as well. For even more quick hits of joy throughout the day, you could have a picture of this thing on your desk, as the background on your computer, or as the wallpaper on your phone.

Smile

Studies have shown that smiling can improve your mood, reduce stress, and even give your immune system a boost. Smiling encourages the production of certain hormones in the brain, such as dopamine and serotonin. Dopamine boosts our feelings of happiness, and serotonin is associated with reduced stress. As you're taking your breaths and visualizing something you love, allow a great big smile to spread across your face.

What if you're having an off day and don't feel like smiling? What if you have to force it? If that's the case, don't worry. A study from the University of South Australia discovered that even a forced smile works on a psychological level (Marmolejo-Ramos et al., 2020). Just the act of smiling itself is enough to improve your mood, reduce stress, and help you achieve an excellent state of mind.

Dial!

Now that you've achieved an optimal state, dialing those numbers and making that call will feel so much easier.

Let's recap the five-step process:

1. **Sit up straight with strong, confident posture**
2. **Take two physiological sighs**—double inhale through the nose, single exhale through the mouth
3. **Visualize something that brings you joy**
4. **Smile**
5. **Make the call, baby! Let's goooo!**

EXTRA TOUGH CALLS

We sometimes have to make calls that we dread. Have you ever phoned a person who's so difficult and disagreeable that you'd rather swim with sharks while bleeding than talk to them? There's usually not much you can do to avoid those conversations. If it's part of your job, it needs to be done. For these special calls, there is a bonus technique that can make these types of interactions easier.

Close your eyes and imagine yourself going through every step of the phone call. Picture yourself handling every question and objection with Obama-like charisma and control. The person seems to be in a better mood and less combative than usual. Imagine the entire call flowing smoothly and effortlessly from start to finish. It feels good, doesn't it?

If you go into the call having just imagined it going well, you'll have different expectations and will therefore approach the conversation differently. Doing this can actually change the outcome of the phone call in your favor. It may sound a little "woo-woo," but it's helped me and countless others before difficult conversations, so it's worth experimenting with. The better you feel as you imagine the call, the more positive the impact.

Keep in mind that you can use both the five-step process and the bonus technique before any type of communication, whether it's face-to-face, video calls, presentations, or meetings. It even helps if you apply it before writing emails to other people.

By putting yourself in this state, you'll be more relaxed, confident, and optimistic. You'll have a sharper, clearer mind, and you'll be able to communicate more effectively at a higher level. All of this will significantly improve your odds of achieving massive amounts of success.

ELITE FOCUS

It's important that you eliminate all distractions and concentrate exclusively on the call. Close your email and minimize all windows. There should be nothing distracting on your screen; the only thing visible should be the other person's picture, and if needed, your bulleted list of talking points for the call.

Turn off notifications on all your devices so you don't have anything popping up and stealing your attention. You may feel the urge to momentarily shift your attention and do a super quick check-in on your emails or texts, particularly if the other person is droning on in a monotone voice and keeps repeating themselves. Do your best to resist this urge and stay fully present and engaged. Depending on your interest level and the nature of the call, this can get *very* challenging.

Embrace the challenge! Each time you find your attention dwindling and you feel the desire to look at something else, try your hardest to bring your focus back to the call. **Like an athlete training for the Olympics, you are training yourself to focus better and actively listen when it gets difficult.**

The ability to stay focused and engaged when your mind wants to wander is a valuable skill in the professional world. So, instead of just being bored on the phone and half-listening, you can choose to view these situations as potent training sessions where you are putting in reps and improving your mental strength.

ALWAYS INCLUDE APPRECIATION

If you'll recall from Chapter 4, **humans want to feel valued, appreciated, understood, and listened to.** This is one of the *most important* things to keep in mind when communicating with another person. When we make people feel this way, they are far more likely to trust us, like us, be receptive to what we have to say, and be more agreeable in our conversations.

Expressing thanks and gratitude to others goes a long way, so every phone call should include some form of appreciation. While we're at it, *every* type of interaction would be better with a little appreciation tossed in.

Appreciation for a person's time is a big one. Our time is extremely valuable, and many of us feel that we don't have enough of it. How many times have you heard some version of "There just aren't enough hours in the day"? Acknowledging someone's time is an excellent way to show that you care about them and recognize their value.

When ending a phone call with someone, thank them for taking the time to speak with you. If you've left a voicemail and someone has called you back, say that you appreciate them returning your call. If someone calls you, begin by thanking them for taking the time to reach out. I've found that people respond exceptionally well to these quick little gratitude statements, which sets a positive, productive tone for current and future communications.

So, never pass up an opportunity to show appreciation. In saying that, I'd like to take a moment to appreciate you, the reader of this book. I appreciate you for taking the time to invest in yourself and improve your communication skills. The fact that you're here right now says a lot about your character.

If you own *Elite Communication Skills for Young Professionals*, that means you genuinely care about making progress in your life. You know you're capable of achieving more, and you're actually doing something about it. A lot of people feel that way but would rather kick it on the couch for another episode instead of taking any action. You're taking action, and I appreciate you for it. You deserve some recognition!

Every moment of gratitude goes a long way in making others feel valued and appreciated. This leads to deeper connections and makes you more likable, which sets you up for more success down the road.

Speaking of being likable, as a reader of this book, you now have the option to gain free access to my online course on likability. If you didn't see it in the beginning pages, the course is called *How to Be Instantly Likable to Fast-Track Your Success (While Still Being Your Authentic Self)*.

If you're interested in watching the course, I set up a page at www.instantlikability.com/free-access (scan the QR code below) that allows readers of *Elite Communication Skills for Young Professionals* to skip the $97 payment step. I'd like to give it to you as a gift of appreciation for buying this book. Your support really does mean a lot to me.

Phew, I'm getting a little emotional writing this. To avoid going any further and becoming that friend that won't stop saying "I love you guys SO much" at the end of a night out, let's move on.

HELLO, IT'S ME

Did you know that **it takes people a tenth of a second to decide whether you're trustworthy when they first meet you?** (Willis and Todorov, 2006).

Similarly, research shows **it only takes people half a second to decide on your trustworthiness when first hearing your voice** (McAleer, Todorov & Belin, 2014).

When it comes to phone calls, that's barely enough time for you to say "hello," which makes how you deliver that greeting incredibly important.

We tend to be the most nervous in the first few seconds of a call, especially when we're caught in the middle of something and not expecting the phone to ring. This often results in a high-pitched, nervous-sounding greeting, which doesn't make an optimal first impression.

Science of People conducted a study where participants recorded "hello" in six different ways. First was a typical "hello" to act as a control. Next, the volunteers recorded the greeting while happy, sad, and angry. They then recorded a "hello" while power posing and finished with another normal "hello" once warmed up.

The researchers concluded that people could sense the emotions in someone's voice even when they only heard *one word* (Science of People, 2020). Just like when making a call, people can tell your emotional state the second you answer the phone. And if your voice conveys negative emotions, people won't like you as much, they'll find you less trustworthy, and your chance of a productive conversation immediately goes way down.

To avoid spitting out a "hello" that sounds like you've just come face-to-face with a T-Rex, don't hold your breath before answering the phone or while waiting for the other party to answer. It causes your vocal cords to tense up, making you sound anxious. Additionally, don't rush to answer the phone when it rings. Doing so can cause you to sound disorganized and impatient. Instead, take a moment to collect yourself and then answer the call.

To collect yourself, you'll want to do a super quick version of the five-step state of mind optimization process. Well, four steps now. There's no "dial" anymore.

When the phone rings, sit up straight, do two quick inhales through the nose, smile, and then answer your phone on the

exhale of that breath. Answering on the exhale instead of the inhale gives off a cooler, more relaxed vocal tone. Smiling is important because, in that same "hello" study, researchers also asked their audience to rate the different greetings based on likability. The highest-rated and most likable "hello" was the happy one that was said while smiling.

Quickly resetting your state of mind this way takes as long as 1-2 rings of your phone, and you'll be surprised by how much of a difference it can make.

FACE-TO-FACE

Even though they are the least used, face-to-face interactions are still the most powerful way to communicate. Speaking in person creates connections that are tough to replicate, and it's the best way to ensure your message is understood and delivered clearly.

While it wouldn't be very efficient (or realistic) to always meet face-to-face, there are times when it's best to do so:

- When you need to build trust
- When starting a new business relationship
- When trying to initiate an important discussion
- When discussing emotional or high stakes topics
- When sharing specific concerns or sensitive information
- If that's what your audience prefers

With so many of us working remotely, there are certainly fewer opportunities to engage in face-to-face interactions. But when it is possible, start prioritizing meeting with others in person, particularly the people that can have an impact on your career.

For example, if you can choose between working from home and going into the office, pop into the office at least once a week to interact with your colleagues and managers. It will go a long way in building relationships and rapport with your team.

When scheduling key meetings with clients or prospects, offer an in-person meeting as the first choice. Make it convenient for them by offering to meet at their office or a location of their choosing. It may take more time, but meeting in person will increase your chances of success with anyone you want to influence.

ACTION STEP

The next time you're tempted to just fire off another email, be a courageous communicator and pick up the phone. Start making more phone calls. You can always send a short summary email after the call if you need a paper trail to follow. And for those important situations when you really want to make an impact, offer to meet face-to-face. **When you choose the types of communication that allow voices to be heard and body language to be seen, it leads to better connections, deeper levels of trust, and stronger relationships.**

CHAPTER 7

WRITTEN COMMUNICATION

❝ *Writing, the art of communicating thoughts to the mind through the eye, is the great invention of the world."*

—Abraham Lincoln

I t's time to put the metaphorical pen to paper. That's right—your next step to becoming an elite communicator is mastering the written word.

According to a study by the National Association of Colleges and Employers, the ability to communicate effectively in writing is a skill that employers highly value. The study found that 73.4% of employers seek out candidates who have strong written communication skills.

The ability to write well is one of the most in-demand skills, and for good reason—writing has become the most common way to communicate in a professional environment.

We spend a large portion of every day writing various emails, messages, reports, and other documents. As we continue to live in the "Information Age," there's too much data constantly being sent around for anyone to remember, which makes written communication an essential part of our daily lives.

With a few simple changes, you can see tremendous results and significantly improve everything you write from this point forward.

By implementing the tactics in this chapter, you will:

- Be able to write clear, powerful, reader-friendly messages
- Have more influence in your company
- Get more respect from everyone who reads your writing
- Save time throughout your workday
- Increase your response rate
- Enhance the quality of replies you receive
- Become more likable to everyone around you

No matter what your professional goals are, written communication is vital to accelerating your progress and maximizing your success.

WHEN TO COMMUNICATE IN WRITING

While we want to avoid hiding behind a screen and being overly reliant on it, there are many times when written communication has its advantages.

Here are some examples:

- When you require a record of the communication to refer back to
- When you need to explain particularly complex information
- When you have to keep track of numerous details
- When you have to communicate with a large number of people
- When you are sending images, charts, statistics, or diagrams

STRATEGIC FOCUS ON THE READER

As with all types of communication, one of the most impactful things you can do when writing is to focus on your audience. Shift your attention away from yourself and think about who will be reading your message.

Before you start writing, consider the following questions:

- Who is my audience?
- How knowledgeable are they about the topic?

- What do they need to know?
- Why should they care?
- What do they need to do after reading?
- When do they need to do it?
- What's in it for them?

As you write, minimize your use of "I" and make your message about the reader as much as possible. If a lot of your sentences start with "I," then it will sound like you're writing more for yourself than the other person, which can be off-putting and reduce the chances of your reader taking action.

Here's a simple example. You're asking for some information, and you write:

"I'd like to have this back by Friday."

Sounds fine, right? You really do want it back by Friday, and you're being clear in your communication. Satisfied, you hit send and move on to the next task.

Little do you know, this is what the recipient might think when they read your message:

"Excuse me, why should I care when you want this back? What's in it for me? I have a lot of other work to do. Do you think you're more important than me? And there's not even a please in there. No manners Nancy back at it again. You are going LOW on the priority list."

To improve the response you get—*and* make the person like you more—this statement could be changed to:

"If you could please have this back by Friday, that would be greatly appreciated. The client is a bit impatient, and we'll increase our chances of getting the deal if we act quickly."

First, we removed the "I" and added a "you" to make it less us about us and more about them. We then tossed in a "please" and added appreciation for a warmer tone. We included reasons why getting it back by Friday would be beneficial, and we spoke in terms of the company and the client (instead of ourselves), which the reader is more likely to care about—especially when compared to us simply saying, *"I want it."*

The word "we" was also strategically used. "We" is inclusive and reminds them that you're on the same team and share the same goals.

If you had said:

"The client is a bit impatient, and I'll increase my chances of getting the deal if you act quickly," then it becomes very individual-focused again. It's like saying, *"You need to do this for **me** so that **I** can get the deal."*

This sounds self-centered and isn't very appealing to the reader. Using "we" in these cases is a subtle change that will increase the effectiveness of your written communication.

ASK, DON'T TELL

There will be many times throughout your career when you need another person to answer your question, gather information, or complete a task for you. In these cases, it's best to avoid directly telling them what to do. If you're always telling people what to do, you will face a lot of resistance.

You might think that ordering people around will get you faster results, but that only works if you're in the military. **If you want things to get done, leave your drill sergeant persona at home and phrase all of your demands as *questions*.**

The switch to questions is important because there's a part of our brain that simply does not like being told what to do—especially when it's coming from someone who isn't our boss.

Humans want to be independent and autonomous. We want to make the rules and call the shots, which is apparent at almost every stage in our lives.

When we're toddlers, and an adult tells us not to do something, we giggle and do it anyways. As teenagers, we think we've got it all figured out and roll our eyes at our parents' rules. And as adults, many of us still get defensive or irritated when we're told to do something, even if it's for our benefit. Can you think of a time when you just wanted to be heard, and someone jumped in and started blasting you with unsolicited advice? How did you feel?

We all have an inner rebel that resists being told what to do. This inner rebel is your brain reacting to what it perceives as a threat to your freedom. If you're regularly sending emails telling everyone what to do instead of asking for their assistance, you could be creating many annoyed people in your professional life. If someone is annoyed with you and thinks you're ordering them around, they're going to like you less, and they're not going to be motivated to respond.

Advancing your career is a lot more difficult when no one wants to help you. To change this narrative, all you have to do is make a small adjustment—**ask for help instead of giving directions.** This can make a shockingly significant impact on your life. People will want to help you more, they will respond faster, and they will think higher of you.

For example, if you write, *"Provide the following information."* Most people will interpret this as cold, direct, and think you're trying to be an authority figure giving them orders.

You're better off changing it to, *"Would you please provide the following information?"*

By adding warmth, respect, and turning it into a question, the reader will respond more constructively and likely send you the information much faster.

THE POWER OF "WOULD YOU MIND"

Another great alternative for this statement is, *"Would you mind providing the following information?"*

"Would you mind" is an excellent way to ask for something, and it can be especially useful with the more difficult people in your world. With this phrase, answering "no" really means saying "yes."

Because *"No, I wouldn't mind,"* or *"No, I don't mind,"* actually mean *"Yes, I'll do it,"* **this is a sneakily effective way to ask for something from a person who loves saying no or has a reputation of being difficult.**

Because the word "no" comes into their mind, they subconsciously feel in control and are more likely to respond favorably to your request. Isn't the brain fascinating?

If you know a person is particularly busy, stressed, or if they're a little more sensitive than others, you could also add in, *"When you have a moment,"* or *"If it's not too much trouble,"* before your question.

These words are generally very well received from people in those situations because they show an added level of respect for the other person and their time. If we add these to our example, it will sound like this:

> *"When you have a moment, would you mind providing the following information?"*

> *"If it's not too much trouble, would you mind providing the following information?"*

Everyone at work will immediately like you more if you start showing more respect in your written communication. And like many of the communication tips you are learning, this is useful to implement in your personal life as well. If you want your friends, family, or significant other to respond more positively to your requests—**ask, don't tell.**

LEAVE NO TONE UNTURNED

Do you ever hear voices in your head? You may be hearing one right now, and it's reading these words to you. Hopefully, the voice you hear is yours, and if it isn't, I hope it's at least a pleasant one. Like a deep, soothing Morgan Freeman voice. Do you hear *his* voice now?

No matter whose voice you hear, your brain will naturally assign a tone to that voice based on the words, which is why it's absolutely crucial to be mindful of your tone when you're writing. Tone is just as important in writing as it is in verbal communication.

Take the following sentence as an example:

> *"You clearly weren't listening because this is not what I need."*

How does it sound? Even if you read it in Morgan Freeman's majestic voice, you're still probably hearing an angry (or at least irritated) tone in your mind. Now, as the receiver of that message, you're likely annoyed and thinking some version of, *"I don't think so, peabrain. You clearly didn't explain it well enough."*

Let's take a different approach to deliver the same message:

> *"Thanks for taking the time to send this. If it's not too much trouble, would you mind sending over the other part as well? I apologize if I wasn't clear enough in my first request. Much appreciated!"*

Sounds a lot better, doesn't it? Unlike the first message, it certainly doesn't sound like the sender is three seconds away from ripping your head off. Now, you're more likely to think something along the lines of, *"Oh, that's okay, it could have been my fault too. Here's the other part you need."*

To some of you, the second version of the message might sound a little over the top on the "nice" scale. There's a reason behind this. Particularly in professional settings, it's far too common for the tone of a person's writing to be negatively misinterpreted, so if you want someone to complete a task for you, it's better to be a little extra positive.

One of the greatest benefits of writing in a positive tone is its impact on your likability. No one wants to read another negative message from Grumpy Gary or Sour Susan. When you send upbeat messages written in a positive tone of voice, you will automatically become more likable.

Studies have shown that the more well-liked a person is, the more likely they are to get promotions, pay increases, and see faster career jumps—and this is *regardless* of the person's education level or professional qualifications. Likable people get more useful information about projects, receive higher quality feedback, and get more help from others when they need it.

If you've had a chance to watch your free gift—my likability course—you already know how to be more likable in your everyday life. Now, to help you boost your likability specifically in your writing, let's look at some more examples of positive vs. negative tones.

You write:

> *"If you don't get me the numbers by tomorrow, we won't make the deadline."*

How's the tone? A bit gloomy?

This sentence could be improved by saying:

> *"If you send me the numbers by tomorrow, we will be able to submit the report on time."*

Notice how we removed the "don't" and "won't" and rewrote the sentence to enhance the tone, making it sound more positive and increasing the chances of it being well-received.

As a general rule of thumb, if you can change a "don't, won't, or can't" into a "do, will, or can," it will upgrade the tone of your message.

The idea is to say what something *is* instead of what something *isn't*. By doing so, **we are focusing on solutions instead of problems.**

Here are two more examples:

> *1. "I can't send you the offer right now because I'm out of town until next week."*

This turns into:

> *"I will send you the offer next week when I get back to the office."*

> *2. "I won't submit the proposal until I get approval from our VP."*

This becomes:

> *"I will submit the proposal when I receive approval from our VP."*

Additionally, if you want to avoid making enemies in the office, never make it sound like the reader is wrong.

So instead of:

"You made a mistake in the document."

Flip it to:

"There seems to be a mistake in the document."

This is when you'll want to refrain from using the word "you." You know you have to point out the mistake, but why not let the person save face and maintain your relationship with them?

These small changes can have a big impact on how others perceive you. Keep an eye on your communication style as you write, and if you find that you frequently use negative terms, make an effort to replace them with more positive ones.

If you're unsure about your tone in an email, try reading it objectively as if you had just received it from someone else. For those extra important emails, you can ask a friend or co-worker to give it a quick read to see how they interpret your tone before you send it.

Moreover, it can be useful to read your writing out loud to see how it sounds. Reading your writing aloud will also help you improve the clarity of your message and make it sound more natural.

There are certain nuances of tone to consider when writing in our professional lives, but when it comes to our personal lives, we have it so much easier. If we're sending a text to a friend, we have one of the most effective modern communication tools for portraying tone at our disposal—*emojis*. With a vast and ever-increasing array of emojis to use, we have the incredible luxury of adding virtually any tone to the messages we send.

We can even use multiple emojis in a row to show emphasis. Exactly how much emphasis? That's up for interpretation. Three crying laughing emojis in a row used to pack a lot of punch, but now it seems to be a fairly common response to anything slightly humorous.

And GIFs! Messaging gets taken to a whole new level when we incorporate GIFs. Let's say you've been waiting a long time for your boss to answer an important email from last week. Imagine sending them an email saying, *"Following up on this…"* along with the *"It's been 84 years"* GIF from the Titanic to emphasize how long it's taken them to respond. Hilarious, sure, but not something you can do in a professional setting.

Because we can't use emojis and GIFs as we do in our personal messaging, and the reader cannot hear our voice, see our facial expressions, or pick up on our body language, we need to be particularly mindful when it comes to the tone of our writing.

KISS

Communicating in writing is all about the words you use. If you're using a lot of buzzwords and complicated terms, you could end up looking insincere or overly salesy.

A study on the impact of linguistic concreteness discovered that people considered content more honest and trustworthy when the writer used concrete language instead of abstract language (Hansen & Wänke, 2010). **Essentially, if you write in simpler language, there's a higher chance your words will be perceived as true.**

On the other hand, if you go out of your way to use complicated, multisyllabic words in hopes of sounding intelligent, you'll be deemed as less trustworthy (and possibly pretentious). Wait, should I not have used the word "multisyllabic"?

Some folks on LinkedIn love to do this in their communications, thinking it will help them build authority and increase their status, but they don't realize that their core message often gets buried between their over-the-top word choices.

If you want people to understand you and believe in your message, keep it short and simple.

EASY ON THE EYES

One of the kindest, most considerate things you can do for others is to make your emails and messages easy to read. And easy to read *quickly*.

Imagine opening an email and seeing nothing but five massive blocks of text. There are about ten lines per paragraph. No spacing. Just words on words on words. How do you feel looking at this monstrosity of a message? I just shuddered at the very thought of it. Sounds like a "delete, claim you never received it, and hope for the best" type of email.

Your goal when writing is to do the opposite of this. To save yourself loads of time and make sure people actually read your words, only write what's absolutely necessary. There's no need to spend time writing six paragraphs when two will get your point across.

In order to keep the reader's attention and make the text easier to read on a screen, you want to increase the white space by keeping your paragraphs short—two to three sentences in an email, a maximum of five in a document.

You can even have one sentence stand on its own for emphasis.

Speaking of sentences, we want those to be short as well. Do your best to keep them as clear and concise as possible. Everyone will appreciate you for it.

Using bullet points is another excellent way to create white space and boost the readability of your messages. Any time you're listing more than one thing, you can *shoot some bullets* into your writing.

Bullets help:

- Make your message easier to read
- Your words stand out clearly
- Organize your message

It also helps that bullets force you to use concise language instead of a bunch of extra details. If you've got large chunks of text, try to break a few of them down into bullet points to shorten your message and make it easier to consume.

STRUCTURING YOUR EMAILS

Now, let's start writing an email and break down the structure of an optimized message. We'll begin at the very top.

THE SUBJECT LINE

The subject line should be clear, specific, and communicate exactly what the email is about. The receiver should be able to prioritize the email's importance without opening it.

Subject lines might not seem like a big thing, but when you think of the thousands of emails we receive, anything with a non-descriptive subject can get overlooked and then buried in the email abyss. Your subject line needs to be searchable so it's easy to find for both you and the recipient in the future.

Sending a vague subject line like *"Proposal"* or *"Request for Information"* will make your message difficult to find down the road. After all, which proposal is this? What information are you requesting?

Instead, use a subject line like, *"Your Company Name Proposal for Their Company Name"* or *"Request for Information on 420 Green St. Venue."*

When they want to refer back to it, they can search *"Your Company Name Proposal"* and find it right away. If you just titled it *"Proposal"* they'd have to scroll through every email with the word proposal in the title.

Small things like this are important for your success. High-level professionals like to do business with people who make their lives easier and help them be efficient, not people who create extra work for them.

THE GREETING

Begin every email by mentioning the recipient's name and including a greeting.

- *Hi Nolan,*
- *Good morning Jesse,*
- *Good afternoon Brook,*

This is the most common way of writing greetings, but if you want to get technical, the correct way of writing this from a grammatical perspective is with another comma in between the greeting and the person's name.

- *Hi, Nolan,*
- *Good morning, Jesse.*
- *Good afternoon, Brook,*

These greetings are considered more formal in nature, and both ways are acceptable. Which style you choose will depend on who you're sending the message to and how formal you want to be.

What if you're writing to multiple people? If you're sending an email to 1–3 people, list each of their names in the greeting. If there are more than three people, it starts looking a little funny to write them all out, so use a greeting such as *"Hello all,"* or *"Hi everyone,"* or address their group, such as *"Hi Marketing team,"* or *"Hello AGI team."*

Finally, it's best to refrain from using *"Hey"* in a professional email. Even if it might be safe to send *"Hey Evan,"* to your best work pal, it's better to avoid getting into the *"Hey"* habit. It's just a little too casual and not worth the risk of sounding unprofessional.

THE PLEASANTRY

After your greeting, add a quick pleasantry, which is a 'pleasant remark made to be polite." This is a great way to add some warmth right off the bat and enhance the tone that the rest of your email will be read in.

Here are three examples of pleasantries to use in your rotation:

- *I hope you're doing well.*
- *I hope you're having a great week.*
- *I hope you enjoyed your weekend.*

If the conversation has already started, your pleasantry rotation would sound like this:

- *Thanks for your message.*
- *Thanks for getting back to me.*
- *I appreciate your quick response.*

As Vinay Patankar explains on the *Abstract Living* blog, *"You should ALWAYS follow with a pleasantry after your greeting. EVERYTIME without fail. Ingrain this into your fingers so that you naturally spit it out with each email you write ... You will never have anything to lose by adding in a pleasantry, you will make people more inclined to read the rest of your email, you will soften criticism, and will hit the positive emotions of a few. Most will simply ignore it, but for two seconds of your time, it's definitely worth it."*

It's true—all of these little things add up when it comes to being more likable at work and gaining more influence over others.

THE BODY

If the goal of your email is to explain something, structure the body of your email with a framework you're already familiar with—the PREP framework.

Here's a quick summary of **PREP** to refresh your memory:

- **Point**—state your point (*what* you think)
- **Reason**—the reason behind your point (*why* you think it's true)
- **Evidence**—give evidence/examples to support your reasoning (*how* you know it to be true)
- **Point**—restate your point (*what* you think)

Depending on the email, you may need to add a call to action (CTA). A successful CTA outlines the reader's next steps and gets them to take action.

This is when you would ask strategically phrased questions like the ones from earlier in the chapter:

- *Would you mind providing the following information?*
- *Would you please send those files by end of day Thursday?*
- *Would you mind reaching out to Braedon and booking a meeting for next week?*

Make sure to include *when* you'd like the action completed if you need something done within a certain time frame.

If you're sending a longer email that includes information on various topics, the body of your message will be structured differently.

Begin by introducing the main subject and providing background information. List each topic, explain them individually, summarize each topic, and finish with a CTA if needed.

If you're replying to an email that includes multiple questions, listing your answers *by themselves* at the top of a new email isn't the reader-friendly move. Instead, after your greeting and pleasantry, write *"Please see answers below in blue"* or red, or bold—whatever you prefer that will make them stand out. Then, copy and paste the questions from the original email and write your answers beside them in blue or whatever you chose. If I decided to write my answers in bold, it would look like this:

When can I expect to see results? **Most clients start noticing changes within the first 2 weeks of the program.**

Is there a payment plan? **Yes, you have the option of splitting the cost over six monthly payments.**

What if it doesn't work? **As long as you commit to showing up 1 hour per week and implementing what you learned, I promise you will see tremendous changes in your life. We're so confident that we offer multiple guarantees:**

1. **100% Money Back Guarantee—you can ask for a full refund of your money at any point during the program. No questions asked, and no hard feelings!**
2. **100% Satisfaction Guarantee—if you're not 100% satisfied at the end of the program, Ty will keep working with you for free until you are. This sounds crazy to some people, but that's how important your success is to us.**

(Note: I copied this from an email exchange my Support Team had with a client.)

When you write this way, they can clearly see your answers right beside their questions, which saves them from jumping back and forth between emails. This makes it noticeably easier for them to follow and understand.

THE CLOSING

Your closing should be just as warm and powerful as your opening. Remember, you're trying to build strong relationships with the people reading these emails, so it's important to leave them with a favorable impression of you.

Any version of *"Thank you"* or *"Regards"* is generally a safe bet when ending a message—it's tough to go wrong with any of these. That being said, variety is the spice of life, even with email closers. Depending on the situation, I'll sometimes mix it up and finish in a different way, such as:

- *Looking forward to this!*
- *Looking forward to working with you.*
- *Happy to answer any questions.*
- *Let's do this!*

If you work in sales and send a lot of cold emails, your messages should always end with thanks and appreciation. A study that analyzed more than 350,000 email threads discovered that messages closing with some form of gratitude had a whopping 36% higher response rate than any other closing (Boomerang, 2017). In case you're wondering, *"Best,"* had the lowest response rate.

In general, it's especially important to show gratitude when someone has just performed a task for you or sent something you know took time or effort. They deserve recognition and appreciation each and every time.

Here are some closing statements for you to use in those situations:

- *Thanks for your time.*
- *Your help is greatly appreciated.*
- *Thank you for everything.*
- *I appreciate your help.*

Some of my 1-on-1 coaching clients are a bit cynical and struggle with this at first, which is completely understandable. Especially when it comes to work, they'll say things like:

> *"Well, that person only does this task because it's their job. I don't believe they're doing it for me. Why should I give extra appreciation to someone for simply doing what's expected of them?"*

Totally fair. I can *appreciate* this type of thinking (ha). Sure, they may just be doing their job, but giving them consistent appreciation will make them like you a lot more, so they'll be more likely to listen to you, talk you up to others, and help you out much faster.

If you want to rapidly advance your career, having that type of support from the people around you is worth its weight in gold.

ACTION STEP

Pick a day this week and schedule 30 minutes to take a cold, hard look at your sent email folder. Throw on your analytical hat, inquisitive glasses, and pour a glass of whatever tickles your fancy. The first two are metaphorical, and other than the tickling, the third one is literal.

Here's what you want to look for:

- **Focus**—Does it sound like the focus is on the reader, or is it all about you? Which sentences could be changed to make it more about the recipient?
- **Use of "I"**—How many times did you use "I"? Could you change any of them into "you" or "we" to make your message sound less self-centered?
- **Ask, Don't Tell**—Did you give any instructions that could have been phrased as questions?
- **Tone**—How does the tone of your messages sound? Could you sound warmer, more positive, or more professional?
- **Simplicity**—Are you using unnecessarily large or complex words?
- **Length**—If you were on the receiving end of your emails, would you open them and grimace at their length? Could they be shortened for clarity?
- **Readability**—Are there large blocks of text that make you want to shut down your computer and run away? Could you write shorter paragraphs and use more bullet points?
- **Structure**—Are your subject lines short and specific? Are you using proper greetings and pleasantries? Is the body of your message clear and well organized? Are you ending your emails properly?

Reviewing your written communication each week and making regular adjustments will go a long way in improving your skills. While many of these adjustments may seem small and subtle, they will *significantly* affect how people read and respond to your writing and ultimately have a tremendous impact on your success.

As the quality of your writing increases, so does your value as a professional. Written communication skills are highly sought-after and set you apart from the competition. **Whether you're looking for a different job, trying to get a raise or promotion, or switching to a completely new industry, strong writing is a major key to rapidly advancing your career.**

CHAPTER 8

VIDEO CALLS

❝_I told a joke during my Zoom call, and no one laughed._

It wasn't even remotely funny."

—Unknown

Remote working has been on the rise for many years, but the pandemic completely altered our reality—blasting us into a new work-from-home dominant world.

Many employers used to believe that employees wouldn't be as productive in their homes, so they were reluctant to offer it as an option.

Next thing you know, boom! The pandemic happens, and now even the most skeptical owners have to allow their employees to work from home.

And what's been the major byproduct of working from home? Other than the "no pants" jokes, it's definitely video calls. So. Many. Video. Calls.

The Zoom videoconferencing app experienced a 535% increase in daily traffic in 2020, and there are 300 million people using Zoom for video calls every day. Video calls have become one of the most important and widely used methods of communication in our professional lives.

Fortunately, almost everything you've learned about body language, your voice, speaking up, listening, and phone calls can be used for virtual communication. So, other than the few video-specific tips in this chapter, you're already well-positioned for success.

ZOOM-ZOOM

After face-to-face interactions, video calls are the next best way to connect with your fellow humans at work.

People often tell me that they don't like the way they look on camera, that calls take too much effort, or that they feel awkward and uncomfortable on video. So, they schedule a phone call or try to figure it out over email.

I understand those are more comfortable, but choosing video calls is a better move if you want to optimize your communication. You can connect on a deeper level, get your point across better, read facial expressions and gestures, and build stronger relationships.

According to a recent study on the impact of videoconferencing, 98% of respondents agreed that video calls lead to deeper, stronger relationships—both in and out of the office. Additionally, 89% of those interviewed stated they felt a stronger connection with their co-workers and organization when using them.

Further research revealed that 90% of people think they can get their point across better when everyone can see each other. Of these respondents, 98% believe that this helps improve collaboration, communication, and productivity levels.

I couldn't find any studies on awkward silences, but there's usually less of them on video calls compared to phone calls. Another win for Zoom.

So, how do you improve your communication on camera? How do you look like a million bucks, get your message across, and sound like a natural?

That's what this chapter is all about. With the proper setup and preparation, you can look and sound like a true professional. And when you do, people will automatically perceive you as more competent, credible, and take you more seriously.

Most professionals have never been taught how to increase the effectiveness of their video calls, so you can positively set yourself apart by making a few small changes.

GEAR UP

You don't need to spend a fortune on equipment, but having some basic gear will help make your calls more professional. If you're doing a lot of Zoom-ing, there are a few great investments you can make over time to enhance your virtual interactions.

Depending on your budget, there are lots of websites and apps where people sell their gently used technology. In our modern world, people seem to *love* upgrading their technology when they don't need to, which bodes well for a young professional looking to make financially intelligent purchases.

Facebook Marketplace is a solid option because you can check out someone's profile to get a sense of the type of person you're dealing with. Most Facebook profiles show you enough to make a healthy assumption about whether they're going to be a reasonable, normal (enough) human being, which is all you need for a quick exchange.

WEBCAMS

Using your laptop or desktop's built-in webcam is perfectly acceptable, but if you can, look into getting an external webcam. It makes it a lot easier to create the perfect angle and is worth it for the superior image quality.

MICROPHONES

Depending on your computer, using the built-in microphone and speakers can create feedback on the call and sound like your voice is bouncing around. To make sure your voice sounds clear, do a test call with a friend or co-worker and have them rate the clarity of your voice.

If it needs improvement, even a pair of basic headphones with a mic can give your voice a better sound than a lot of built-in microphones. And if you really want to level up and sound your best, consider a standalone microphone that plugs into your computer.

STANDING DESK CONVERTERS

A standing desk converter is a height-adjustable surface that sits on top of your desk, and it can be raised to transform your current work station into a standing desk. They're about 1/5th the price of a normal standing desk, give you all of the same benefits, and can be used on any surface. My standing desk converter has been an absolute game-changer for my workdays in a few different ways:

Improved mood and energy levels: A study conducted over a seven-week period showed that participants using standing desks experienced less stress and fatigue than people who sat throughout their workday (Pronk, Katz, Lowry & Payfer, 2012). Furthermore, 87% of the participants who used standing desks claimed to experience greater levels of energy and vigor. When you have higher energy levels and less fatigue, it's easier to focus and maximize your productivity.

Confident body language: When standing, it feels much easier to maintain confident body language—standing tall and straight, head up, shoulders down and back. When sitting, I find I'm more likely to slouch or hunch forward. Anything you can do to make it easier to keep strong body language is a great advantage.

Reduced back and neck pain: Alright, this may not have anything *directly* to do with communication, but I do care about your overall well-being, so it's worth noting for the stiff-bodied chair-sitters out there. Studies have shown that after several weeks of using a standing desk, participants experienced up to a 32% improvement in lower back pain. Another study by the CDC discovered that using a combo of sitting and standing decreased upper back and neck pain by 54% after one month.

If you alleviate some pain and stiffness, you'll likely be in a better mood, making you more likely to have positive interactions at work. Looser body = enhanced communication? We'll roll with it.

WHEN DISASTER STRIKES

Imagine…it's 10:57 a.m., and you have a critical Zoom meeting at 11:00 a.m. Maybe it's a job interview for a position you've always wanted, or you're about to close a lucrative deal with a client.

Suddenly, your internet cuts out. Then your laptop shuts down and refuses to turn back on. And to top it off, your headphones stop working. It's now 10:58 a.m. What do you do?

This is when having backups can save you. It's always a smart idea to have an extra pair of headphones, another device nearby you can use for the call (like your phone), or a mobile data connection (hotspot) you can switch to if your Wi-Fi decides to take a nap.

BACK UP

Sitting too close to the camera is the #1 most common mistake people make on video calls. It's outrageously common, but in all fairness, how many people are ever taught this type of thing? Like many other aspects of communication, we use virtual meetings all the time, and it seems like we're just expected to know what we're doing.

Seeing someone extremely close up—even on screen—looks and feels a bit awkward. The person could be across the world, but it can still feel like they're poking their head through our computer and into our personal space. This is the video call equivalent of the "close talker" in real life.

Additionally, the closer a person is to the camera, the less their body can be seen. Remember the importance of visible hands and hand gestures in the chapter on body language? If you're too close to the camera, only your face can be seen by others. I'm sure that you have a great face, but if your audience can't see anything beyond it, you're missing out on valuable nonverbal cues that will increase connection, charisma, and trust.

Move backward so that you're farther away from the screen and at least the upper half of your torso is visible to your audience. It's crucial that people can see you make those ever-important hand gestures while speaking.

LIGHT UP

Proper lighting is a key ingredient for your professional appearance. To look your best, you're going to want natural light shining on your face from the front. If possible, move your computer in front of a window to get as much natural light as possible. The key is to ensure the light shines straight on your face.

If you don't have a window in your room, you can position a lamp behind your computer or get a light ring to brighten you up. Whether it's fair or not, it's no secret that how you look plays a role in how people judge your credibility. Fixing your lighting is an easy change that can instantly boost your appearance.

LOOK BEHIND YOU

The next professional-looking element to consider is a clean, basic background. The goal is to minimize distractions so that your audience is focused on you and your content.

Have you ever laid awake in bed wondering, *"Is there one particular Zoom background that is widely known as the best?"* I have, so I stayed up late one night trying to find studies and figure out if this "best" background exists. I spent many hours researching, and while I still don't think there is one specific background to rule them all, I did come across an interesting study.

According to the study, people who sit in front of houseplants are perceived as more intelligent, approachable, and trustworthy. Researchers believe houseplants have *grown* in popularity because people have spent less time outside since the pandemic and crave more nature in their lives.

In general, backgrounds with windows and natural lighting also scored well in terms of approachability, intelligence, and trust. As long as there was a window or natural lighting in the frame, people had a more positive perception of the speaker.

Someone once asked me about "R-rated art," so if all the walls in your home are covered in naked pictures, I have a solution for you. Don't worry; I won't ask you to take down your numerous nudes. As a human body enthusiast, I could never do that. The solution for you, my friend, is to invest in a Japanese screen.

A Japanese screen, also referred to as a Shoji screen, is a folding screen traditionally used to divide rooms and provide privacy. It can be set up anywhere in your home, and it immediately turns the space into a clean, professional background that you can put away once you're finished with the call.

While a real background is always preferred, if you're not at home and you're in a pinch, it may be necessary to use a virtual background. Almost all video call platforms allow you to add virtual backgrounds. There are often default backgrounds on the platform itself, or you can add your own image to use. There's no need to spend hours searching for the perfect one—as long as it looks clean and professional with minimal distractions. And because you have the power to do so, you might as well pick a background with a few houseplants in there.

PRIORITIES

According to a survey of video call users, 48% of respondents were more concerned over what they looked like during the call than the content they presented. While looking professional is important, it's not something to *obsess* over.

Once the call starts, your focus should be on delivering value, listening, asking the right questions, and helping others. Just like your meetings and phone calls, you can set yourself up for success with a little preparation. Establish your goals for the call, write out a quick list of talking points to keep yourself on track, then shift yourself into an elevated mental state.

SBVS

Getting into the right state of mind before a video call is just as important as any other interaction. Remember, your state of mind will have a significant impact on your confidence, your voice, your focus, the energy you give off, and how everyone on the call perceives you.

We'll use the same optimization process we used in Chapter 6 before our phone calls—sit up straight, breathe, visualize, and smile. You may notice I took out the "dial" step. Dialing isn't technically part of the preparation process this time, although I did like it for the phone call section because it rhymed with "smile."

Let's recap the 20-second process that will instantly boost your mood:

1. **Sit up straight with strong, confident posture**
2. **Take two physiological sighs**—double inhale through the nose, single exhale through the mouth
3. **Visualize something that brings you joy**
4. **Smile**

To make it easier to remember, think of the acronym **SBVS— Straight, Breathe, Visualize, Smile.**

If you need a little extra boost, you can also add the bonus visualization here. This is where you imagine the entire call going smoothly, picturing yourself handling every question and objection with Oprah-like charisma and control.

Use **SBVS** before your next video call to put yourself in a positive, focused, relaxed state of mind. Notice how much better people respond to you when you join virtual meetings feeling this way. Taking twenty seconds before an interaction can have a huge impact on helping you achieve the results and success you're looking for.

"JUST SMILE AND WAVE"

I didn't plan on mentioning penguins twice in this book, but all I could think of when writing this was the scene in Madagascar when Skipper, Rico, and Private are smiling and waving, trying to look natural, while Kowalski is right behind them digging a tunnel for the gang to escape to Antarctica.

"Just smile and wave, boys. Smile and wave."

— Skipper the Penguin

While the penguins' goals are different than ours, Skipper's advice is strategically sound and should be followed at the beginning and end of every video call. **In a virtual meeting, smiling and waving is the closest thing you can do to replicate a handshake.** It's a gesture of warmth and respect, and it's the most effective way of creating trust and connection when starting a call.

STARING AT YOURSELF

It's not unusual for people to watch themselves while on a video call. According to a study on video call participants, 30% of individuals stated they spent around *half the call* staring at their own faces. Are you one of those people? If you are, I totally understand. It's hard *not* to check yourself out on the screen.

If you think about it, this would be the equivalent of staring at yourself in the mirror while talking with someone in real life. I'm all for self-love, so if you want to make deep eye contact with yourself and say "I love you" into the mirror when you're alone, I support you. But when you're communicating with another person, looking at yourself is distracting, and it will diminish your ability to engage fully, listen actively, and ask the right questions. Essentially, you're not putting yourself in the best position to add value to the discussion.

When speaking, look at your camera—the little dot on the top of your screen. Just like smiling and waving is the video call equivalent of a handshake, looking at your camera is the closest thing you can do to simulate in-person eye contact and encourage the release of oxytocin. If you'll recall from Chapter 6, oxytocin is associated with increased empathy, trust, and relationship-building.

When listening, if you're finding it challenging not to look at your ridiculously attractive self, try switching to "speaker view" instead of "gallery view." Now the person talking is front-and-center, making it easier to watch them and less tempting to look at yourself.

MORE GRATITUDE

Gratitude makes people light up. We all want to be appreciated, and we want that recognition, but many of us feel that we don't get enough of it—at work, at home, in our relationships, friendships, etc. If you show appreciation to someone, you're giving them something they crave on a deep level. Always close your video calls with some version of: *"Thanks for your time today. I really enjoyed speaking with you."*

On top of a verbal thank you at the end of the call, sending a quick message within the first few hours afterward is an extremely likable thing to do. This can be a brief thank you email to everyone on the call, or a short text if you have their numbers and want to add an even more personal touch. It only takes 1 minute, and it has a powerful effect on strengthening your relationships. All you have to say is, *"Great call today, everyone. I really appreciate your time. Looking forward to our next steps!"*

ACTION STEP

It's time to toss on your analytical hat again. Record your next video call and evaluate your performance. It may feel uncomfortable watching yourself on video (for some of you, *really* uncomfortable), but I promise it will pay significant dividends in your career. You can learn so much about yourself doing this, and you'll know exactly what to work on after you finish. Outside of the video call platform itself, you can use programs like OBS or Loom to record your calls for personal review.

I made a checklist for you to help with your analysis. It includes the key ideas from previous chapters with added video-specific tips from this chapter.

- **Your Setup**
  - Camera position—upper torso and hand gestures are visible
  - Clean, professional background
  - Quality lighting—front-facing natural light is best
- **Your Nonverbal Communication**
  - Wave and smile—at the beginning and end of the call
  - Strong, confident body language—shoulders back, head up, back straight
  - Eye contact—looking at the camera when speaking, looking at the speaker when listening, not constantly checking yourself out
  - Appropriate facial expressions
  - Consistent use of hand gestures
- **Your Content**
  - Could you have spent more time preparing and known your content better?
  - Did your audience seem to have a good understanding of what you were saying?
  - Could you have explained anything more clearly using the PREP framework?
- **Your Listening**
  - How would you rate your listening?
  - Could you have asked more open-ended questions?
  - Did you paraphrase others' words back to them to show understanding?
- **Your Voice**
  - Did you sound confident and sure of yourself?
  - Was your tone warm, friendly, and engaging?

- ○ Were there times that you sounded less or more confident, and the volume of your voice decreased or increased?
- • **Gratitude**
  - ○ Did you include appreciation at the end?
  - ○ Did you send a short thank you message after the call?

When you can watch your video calls and consistently check the points off this list, you will have achieved elite virtual communication status, and you will be exceptionally well-positioned to move up in the world.

CHAPTER 9

PRESENTATIONS

" *According to most studies, people's number one fear is public speaking. Number two is death. Death is number two. Does that sound right? This means to the average person, if you go to a funeral, you're better off in the casket than delivering the eulogy."*

—Jerry Seinfeld

n this chapter, we'll be tackling a skill that can single-handedly launch your career to new heights—giving powerful presentations. We'll talk about the fear of public speaking and why presentation skills are so essential, and then we'll dish out an enormous buffet of tips to take your presentations to the next level.

THE FEAR OF PUBLIC SPEAKING

If public speaking ever makes you nervous, you are not alone. It's one of the most common fears among people—more common than the fear of death, spiders, and heights. The National Institute of Mental Health reports that public speaking anxiety, also known as glossophobia, affects about 73% of the population.

This fear is *so* common that when studies are done on stress, researchers will use it to induce anxiety in their participants—simply by *asking them to give a speech*.

Just like our suspicion of hidden hands and our hesitation to speak up, many experts believe this fear comes from evolution. If you'll recall from Chapter 3, when humans lived outdoors and had to hunt for food, we had a greater likelihood of survival if we were part of a group. So, our instincts told us to do whatever it takes to be accepted by the tribe.

These instincts still remain inside of us, contributing to our fear of public speaking because we don't want to be isolated or rejected. This makes sense, because when we're presenting, we're usually standing alone at the front of a room or sitting alone in front of a computer. And we're usually the only one speaking. We already feel isolated, and now we're afraid the people watching will judge or reject us, causing even stronger feelings of separation. Instinctually, we still believe this isolation from the group could result in our demise.

Your logical brain knows it's fine, but your instincts are screaming at you that you must be part of the group to survive. So, if you ever get nervous about public speaking, cut yourself some slack and know that it's not your fault. The root cause of this fear has been around for millions of years and is wired into your brain.

Even if the fear always remains on some level, there are many ways for us to effectively manage it and transform ourselves into high-level presenters. You've conquered other difficult things in your life, and you'll be able to overcome this as well.

Like the other communication skills you've been reading about, presenting to groups is a learnable skill that anyone can master. It may get uncomfortable, and it may take more time and effort than some of the other things we've been learning, but I promise it will be worth it. If you're not at elite presentation status *yet*, you will be—all you need to do is keep your learner's mindset and follow this chapter.

THE IMPORTANCE OF PRESENTATION SKILLS

There was once a time when CEOs and top managers were the only ones expected to give presentations. Now, in the modern professional world, almost everyone (regardless of their role) needs to be able to explain information and deliver presentations—internally to their organization and externally to customers and clients.

According to a survey conducted by Prezi, 70% of US employees consider presentation skills essential to their success (many experts believe the other 30% just don't know it yet). Despite most people understanding the importance of presentations, 20% stated they would go to great lengths to avoid giving one, such as asking a colleague to replace them or pretending to be sick. The fear of presenting is all too real among today's professionals, so much so that some people are desperate to get out of it.

Because it can be so uncomfortable, a lot of professionals don't take much time to learn, practice, and develop these skills. This means that presentation skills can be a primary differentiator among you and your peers, giving you a huge competitive advantage. If you master your presentation skills, you will become the master of your career options.

Let's look closer into the benefits of improving your presentation skills.

1. **You become memorable**—When you're a great presenter, people remember you for the right reasons. They won't remember the person reading their slides word for word in a monotone voice, but they will remember the person who knows how to connect with their audience, keep everyone engaged, and explain information in a meaningful and interesting way.

2. **People will want to implement your ideas**—When you know how to explain your ideas properly, there's a significantly higher chance they will be put into action. You know your audience, you tailor your message based on who you're speaking to, and you specifically highlight what's in it for them.

3. **You will be seen as an asset to the company**—Most of us start by presenting internally to our organization and to the smaller, less important clients. The more success you have in

these situations, the more you become an asset to the company and chosen to take on higher-value opportunities.

4. **You're more likely to get promoted**—As you take on these larger opportunities, your value to the organization increases, drastically improving your chances of being promoted. Your position in the company will naturally advance to match your new level of output.

5. **You will expand your network**—If you can captivate and fully engage your audience when presenting, people will notice. They'll start speaking highly of you and telling others about your ideas. One solid presentation can create a domino effect and lead to all kinds of new connections—people who might want your advice, your services, or for you to come work for them.

6. **You can land your dream job**—Whether it's moving up in your current company, crushing it during a huge job interview, or being recruited by someone in your network, presentation skills can be the deciding factor when it comes to landing your dream job.

THE KEYS TO A POWERFUL PRESENTATION

In previous chapters, we covered many aspects of communication that you will continue using to deliver an excellent presentation:

- **Confident posture and body language**
  - If possible, avoid standing behind podiums or anything else that can block the audience from seeing your open body language.
- **Visible hands and use of hand gestures**
  - The highest-rated TED Talk speakers used the most hand gestures.

- **Eye contact**
  - When speaking to a group, pick one person at a time to focus on. Choose one person to look at when explaining a thought, and then switch to another person when you start a new sentence.
- **Appropriate facial expressions**
  - Show interest and enthusiasm, and be mindful of potential "resting witch face."
- **Using your voice effectively**
  - Remember your warm and confident tone of voice, along with your varying voice inflection (upward inflection for questions, downward inflection for serious statements).
- **Explain points clearly with the PREP framework as needed**
  - Point, Reason, Evidence, Point
- **For virtual presentations:**
  - Clean, professional background
  - Quality lighting (front-facing natural light is best)
  - Camera position (upper torso and hand gestures are visible)

Those tactics alone are so powerful, if you follow them, you can get away with below-average content and still have a good presentation.

But is your goal to be just "good," or is it to be exceptional? Did you buy a book called *Decent Communication Skills for Young Professionals,* or are you reading *Elite Communication Skills for Young Professionals?* Would you like to walk down the path to goodness, or would you rather race down the path to greatness?

It's pretty hard to give an elite presentation if your content is dull and bores the pants off of everyone. So, let's dive in and fully immerse ourselves in how to give an excellent presentation.

KEEP YOUR AUDIENCE TOP OF MIND

Nancy Duarte is a presentation expert who has built a career helping people express their ideas in presentations. She is the author of books such as *Slide:ology*, *Resonate*, and *The HBR Guide to Persuasive Presentations*.

According to Duarte, **the most critical part of giving a great presentation is to keep your audience top of mind.** When creating your content, always be thinking about who your audience is. Work on being empathetic towards their preferences, needs, and wants.

One of the most important things to remember is that *you* are not your audience, so what *you* want to see isn't as important. Normally, we create things based on our own preferences and what we like ourselves, and we do this without even thinking. This is cool if you're expressing yourself through art or music, but when you're giving a presentation, it's specifically for the benefit of the people listening, so the most important thing is the value *they* can get from it.

In order to know how to deliver them the most value, we'll need to know more about them. Let's delve into a series of questions that will help you get to know your audience.

What Are They Like?

Start with the demographics of your audience. Look into where they went to school, what departments they work for, their job titles, and their ages. Once you know this base level of information, it's helpful to reach out to someone from your audience to gain more insight.

For example, let's say you work in the accounting department, and you have to make a presentation to the marketing team. You would usually start off discussing facts, figures, and statistics because that's how *your* mind works. But it's not about you, it's about your listeners, so it's best to have a quick chat with someone from marketing to better understand the team's preferred communication style.

You might learn that immediately throwing numbers at them would make them lose interest and that it's better to open with high-level ideas. Maybe they even give you a colorful slide template their team likes to use, and you're told if you have to show data, first explain how it directly relates to their department.

Simple background information like this can do wonders to help you create a presentation that delivers results.

Why Are They Here?

Think of all the meetings, webinars, or seminars you've attended simply because you "had" to. Now, think of a time you've paid money to watch or listen to something you're actually interested in. Take a look at your audience and determine which category they're in—are they there because they *want* to be or because they *have* to be?

It's important to understand what's motivating their attendance. Consider questions such as:

- What are they hoping to get out of the presentation?
- Why are they attending?
- Is their attendance voluntary or not?

Imagine you're sitting on an airplane, and it's about to take off soon. The flight attendants walk to their spots and start the classic pre-flight safety presentation. The information is important, but you've seen it before, and you're not on the plane to watch the presentation. You're there to travel to a new destination via this giant mechanical bird that soars through the sky.

Some airlines have recognized that their audience isn't there to learn about safety, so they've taken extra measures to encourage people to watch and listen. For example, Virgin America's safety video includes humor, pop-culture references, and music, and it's so entertaining that people often want to watch it more than once.

Just like Virgin America, when you know *why* the audience is there, you can adjust your presentation in a way that speaks to them and keeps them interested.

How Can You Help Them?

Knowing your audience's pain points will help you craft your message. What are their problems? What are their frustrations? This information provides valuable context as you create your presentation and develop the tone of your content.

As is human nature, your audience will be listening to you and wondering, *"What's in it for me?"* As you're creating your presentation, make sure you answer that question. Explain how you can make something better for them or help with one of their problems.

Even if your audience really likes you, chances are, they didn't come just to *see* you; they came to *learn* from you.

And whenever possible, back your ideas up with supporting evidence from external sources. Even if you're an expert on the topic at hand, people will always find you more credible.

What Do You Want Them to Do?

What is your goal for the presentation? If everything went exactly the way you wanted, what would the end result be?

Do you want your audience to move to the next step of the sales process? Would you like them to sign up for a course? Do you need their buy-in on a big project? Want them to start using your new system?

If you can clearly show the significant value and benefits of "what could be," you'll have some initial motivation from your listeners. However, that motivation will quickly vanish if there is no clear action plan.

If you want the best possible outcome for your presentation, you need to close out with a call to action (CTA). Avoid overwhelming your audience with too many CTAs; only include one or two simple steps that will create the most forward momentum.

What Objections Might They Have?

Change can be difficult for people, no matter what the situation is. When you ask your audience to make a change, there's likely to be at least some resistance initially, so it's important to come prepared. Think in advance what their objections might be, and plan how you will respond.

One approach is to use empathy and get your listeners to focus on how your idea will make things better. For example, if you're making a case for increased automation, explain how you understand it's a financial investment. Then, focus on the fact that it will mean more time for everyone to work on their most impactful projects. The investment will be worth it to help drive the business forward.

It's also a good idea to allocate time to address your audience's concerns directly. If possible, include a Q&A portion so people can bring up their questions. This gives everyone the chance to speak their mind and allows you to use your listening and mirroring skills on each person individually, making it easier to win them over.

BE A GIVER

If you approach your presentations (and your life) with a giving mentality, you will be amazed at the level of success you can achieve. A giving mentality means that your focus is on offering and providing value rather than taking it. For example, **when you deliver a presentation, you're not telling people to do something so *you* can benefit; you're showing them how *they* can benefit and what *they* can gain from listening to you.**

In other words, you are delivering a presentation because you want to offer your audience something of value—not because you want something from them. You genuinely want to help them. Think of yourself like a teacher.

Even if you're presenting to a boss or a very important person (who, in theory, could help you a lot), being a giver will still get you further than focusing on what you can gain from them. When you take this approach authentically, you will find that people are more drawn to you and your ideas, and you will see significantly better results.

EMOTION + LOGIC = DECISION

Stories are at the heart of our civilization. Since the beginning of time, we've used stories to pass down valuable information to the next generations.

Research shows that our brains are extremely receptive to stories. As we listen to them, it's easy for us to feel as if we're in the story ourselves, experiencing the emotions of each of the characters. During a presentation, stories are a great way to grab people's attention and get them emotionally invested in your content.

Statistics and facts lend more credibility to the ideas in your presentation, and while they're incredibly effective at backing up your points, they have a higher chance of being forgotten compared to stories. People are far more likely to remember a story you told them, especially if there's emotion involved.

For example, let's say you're giving a presentation on how improving the customer experience will benefit your company. Your goal is to get senior management to give employees more freedom and discretion when providing excellent customer service.

To support your point, you offer the following statistics:

- 84% of businesses that invest in providing a better customer experience see an increase in revenue.
- 73% of people say good customer service is important when determining their loyalty to a brand.

- 86% of consumers will pay more for a product or service if it means a better customer experience.

These are all accurate statistics, and they do a solid job of proving your point. Now, if you really want to drive your point home, reinforcing it with a story will make it even more memorable. To go along with your stats (and sticking with our airline theme from the last example), you could share the story of Kerry Drake and United Airlines.

Kerry's mother was on her deathbed, and he was flying to see her one final time before she passed away. As if this wasn't tough enough, his first flight ended up getting delayed. He was now going to miss his connecting flight and would no longer get the chance to say goodbye to his mother.

He broke down crying on the plane and fought through tears to explain his situation to the flight attendants. They shared his story with the captain, who radioed the flight crew of his connecting flight and asked them to wait. The crew's hearts went out for Kerry, and they delayed their departure until he arrived and got on board.

Kerry made it on time to see his mother and was able to say goodbye to her before she passed a few hours later. He was overwhelmed with gratitude for the United Airlines staff and shared the story all over social media.

If those airline employees had to stick to a schedule and couldn't use their discretion, Kerry wouldn't have been able to see his dying mother. The positive press did wonders for United Airlines and shows how important it is to give staff the freedom to use their judgment in special customer service situations.

If I phoned you tomorrow and asked you what percentage of people say good customer service is important when determining their loyalty to a brand, would you know the answer? What if I called and asked what happened to Kerry Drake on United Airlines? What would you remember?

Humans tend to make decisions based on emotion, and then we use logic to justify those decisions. When you're presenting, you can maximize your success by appealing to both sides—the emotional side with stories and the logical side with facts and statistics. This is a powerful way of inspiring people to take action.

For example, if you're trying to get somebody to buy a product from you, tell a story describing how someone's life changed after buying it, creating emotion and painting a picture of what your listener's future could look like. Afterward, you can share data and explain the benefits more in-depth to logically reinforce the decision.

CONTRAST BETWEEN PRESENT & FUTURE

An excellent way to maintain audience engagement and excitement throughout your presentation is to use contrast. In this case, **contrast means describing your audience's current (less than ideal) state and comparing it with a future (more desirable) state—a state they could experience if they go along with your idea.** Contrast clearly illustrates the value that a person could receive and the changes they could see if they move forward with your call to action.

DEFINE YOUR MAIN IDEA

To maximize the success of your presentation, pick *one* key takeaway that you want your audience to leave with, and focus on this *one* main idea. **The main idea should be boiled down into one sentence that sums up your core message, and every element of your presentation should work towards supporting that message.**

If someone from your audience is later asked, *"What was that presentation about?"* This one-sentence main idea is what you'll want them to remember. Using our previous example, you wouldn't say your presentation was about *"The importance of the customer experience."* That's more of a topic than a main idea. Instead, you would say, *"We will see an increase in our revenue, customer loyalty, and public perception if we commit to improving the customer experience."*

Once you've nailed down your main idea, gather as much supporting evidence and material as possible. It's helpful to have plenty of stories, numbers, and facts to choose from when it's time to assemble the final product.

If this sounds overwhelming, don't think you have to do everything from scratch. There's no need to reinvent the wheel. You can look at other presentations, news articles, surveys, industry studies, and any other relevant content connected to your main idea. As much as possible, try to look at anything you find from a few different perspectives and see if you can generate a fresh take on it.

LEBRON AS A SUPERMODEL?

Metaphors, similes, and analogies are incredibly effective at helping people quickly understand new or complicated concepts. They help people connect something new to something they already know and understand.

Let's check out an example that uses one of my favorite humans of all time—LeBron James. In Charles Wheelan's book *Naked Statistics,* he says, *"The Central Limit Theorem is the LeBron James of statistics—if LeBron were also a supermodel, a Harvard professor and the winner of the Nobel Peace Prize."*

Wheelan wanted to show how powerful, elegant, intelligent, and impactful the Central Limit Theorem is in a way that the average person could comprehend. And it worked well. I know nothing about the theorem, but I certainly know who LeBron James is, what a supermodel is, a Harvard professor, etc.

(Side note: can you imagine if LeBron were all of those things? Charles Wheelan must *really* love that Central Limit Theorem.)

Russel Brunson, Founder of ClickFunnels, talks about using a similar tool in his book *Expert Secrets.* He calls it a "kinda like bridge." Every time he's explaining something that a person may be unfamiliar with, he says, *"It's kinda like…"* and relates it to something people already know.

In *Expert Secrets,* Russel gives the following example: *"In a sales script, I mentioned the word 'ketones,' and I watched as the audience zoned out. I discovered that if they don't know what a word means, they stop paying attention to everything you say afterward. So I started using a 'kinda like bridge' like this: 'Ketones are kinda like millions of little motivational speakers running through your body that give you energy and make you feel awesome.'"*

Incorporating these types of comparisons in your presentation will make it significantly easier for you to explain new or complex ideas to your audience.

ASK RHETORICAL QUESTIONS

Rhetorical questions are questions you ask without expecting an answer. You can use them to emphasize a point or increase engagement during a presentation. Our brains are hardwired to answer questions, so they get your audience thinking and more involved in what you're saying. This is a great way to keep people focused as you speak. You ask the question, pause to give them a moment to answer in their minds, and then move on. Depending on what you asked, your next step may be to answer the question yourself.

For example, instead of always saying, *"This is important because…"* you can increase engagement by occasionally adding a rhetorical question, like this: *"Why is this important? (Pause) This is important because…"*

Here are some more examples of rhetorical questions:

- *Do you know how this idea could work for you?*
- *Have you ever felt this way?*
- *What do you think happened next?*
- *We've all experienced this, haven't we?*
- *So, how can we make this better?*

CREATING YOUR PRESENTATION

YOUR STRUCTURE

Now that we've unlocked the keys to a powerful presentation, let's start creating one. Your first instinct might be to open your computer and launch PowerPoint, but according to Nancy Duarte, our presentation expert from earlier, this isn't the best strategy.

When you immediately jump to PowerPoint or other presentation tools, you're almost forced to think through your presentation linearly, one slide at a time. It's easy to get stuck thinking of the details of each individual slide rather than first focusing on the overall structure of your presentation. Instead, she recommends taking out a set of sticky notes or note cards and writing out all of your ideas—one idea per note. Remember, each idea should contribute to your overall "main idea."

Once you have all the ideas out of your brain and onto the notes, stick them to the wall or put them on the ground so you can see them all together. Next, start grouping them by subtopics. As you group similar ideas together, it will become a lot easier for you to organize your content. You can then arrange and rearrange them until you nail down a structure that makes sense. As you complete this, you might find that some of the ideas you initially wrote down aren't necessary and can be taken out.

YOUR SLIDES

Alright, *now* you can open Powerpoint (or your preferred presentation tool) and get cracking. It's time to create slides that are professional, visually appealing, and easy to follow. Remember, the slides are just a supplement for your presentation—you and your content are the stars of the show.

One Idea Per Slide

Stick to one idea per slide. I've worked with a lot of clients who are terrified of high slide counts, which is understandable. We tend to think that more slides = a longer presentation. But that's not the case. You could spend two hours presenting with 1 huge slide or ten minutes presenting with 25 short slides.

Personally, I've seen both, and guess which one was more enjoyable? Watching 25 slides over ten minutes was *far* more interesting.

It's far better to have many slides—each covering a single idea—than to have a few slides—each packed with 10 ideas. The more content you have on a single slide, the harder it is to follow, and there's a higher chance of your audience getting confused or losing interest. Simplicity is key here. The simpler it is, the easier it will be for your audience to understand.

Visuals to Help Explain Your Ideas

Audiences typically retain around 10% of information when a speaker does nothing but talk during a presentation. But if visuals are included, they retain *55% more information.*

The Social Science Research Network states that 65% of people are visual learners who "need to see what they are learning" (Bradford, 2004). If you want your audience to understand and remember your content as much as possible, be sure to incorporate visuals to help explain your ideas. As you're going through your slides, think of how you can add pictures, graphs, or illustrations to prove your point and emphasize your main message.

Where do you find visuals? If you're looking for a free resource, Pixabay.com is a great space to explore. It has over 1.5 million free images and videos that you can use to spruce up your slides. You can also add visual appeal to your presentation using Canva, which has a ton of free infographics, slide templates, and other design elements you can customize. If you want to take things up a notch, there is a premium version of Canva that has incredibly professional-looking presentation templates. Not necessary by any means, but nice to have as an option.

Trim the Fat

Once you've completed your first draft, go through the content of your slides and "trim the fat," which means get rid of anything that isn't needed. Go through each slide and decide if everything you have is necessary for either a.) getting your message across or b.) keeping your audience engaged. If a point, word, or image doesn't directly contribute to either goal, delete it. A lean presentation is a powerful presentation.

Prepare for Resistance

When reviewing your slides, it's a great time to consider different perspectives and how your audience might respond to each one. As we discussed earlier in the chapter, change can be difficult for people, so if you're asking your audience to make a change, there may be a bit of resistance initially. For this reason, it's important to come prepared. Think in advance what their objections might be, and plan your responses accordingly. It's much easier to handle resistance when you're ready and expecting it.

STARTING YOUR PRESENTATION

Now that your slides are complete and you know how to speak about each one, let's look at how to start your presentation with a boom. This might be one of the most underrated and overlooked aspects of public speaking. If you make a great first impression and start off on the right foot, your entire presentation will flow a lot more smoothly.

WHAT NOT TO DO

Let's start with what *not* to do when opening your presentation. The first thing not to do is mention anything about the technology being used for your presentation. This can make you look nervous, unprofessional, or unsure about what you're doing.

It's a common mistake you may have heard before:

- *Can everyone hear me okay?*
- *How's the microphone working?*
- *My goodness, these lights are so bright!*

The next thing not to do is point out how nervous you are. People think that looking vulnerable in front of their audience will make them seem more approachable, which is true, but mentioning your nervousness should never be the first thing out of your mouth.

Avoid openers like:

- *There are so many of you here. I wasn't expecting this!*
- *So, I'm pretty nervous.*
- *Public speaking isn't really my thing.*

You want to start with a strong opening line to get people's attention. That means nice "thank you" statements don't make the cut here either. Save these for the *end* of your presentation.

- *Thank you for having me today.*
- *Thank you for inviting me to speak.*
- *I appreciate your time today.*

OPTIMAL OPENERS

All of the presentation openers you're about to learn have stood the test of time, and highly successful TED Talks have used each of these with incredible impact. You're welcome to choose whichever one feels most comfortable or best suits your presentation.

A Story

One of the best ways to start a presentation is with a story. Stories engage people's imaginations and immediately get their attention.

Here are a few phrases you can use to introduce your story at the beginning of your presentation:

- *The year was 2010. I had just...*
- *The best thing to ever happen to me was...*

- *There's a reason I'm here. And it starts with a story...*

Your Main Idea

You might choose to open the presentation with your main idea. We like when presenters get straight to the point, so there's value in immediately telling people what you're going to be talking about, especially when you do so in a way that gets them intrigued.

If you look at any of the great TED Talks, you'll find that most speakers try to present their main idea as quickly as possible.

Here's how to open with your main idea:

- *There's one thing you need to know today. And that is...*
- *Today, I'm going to share something important with you...*
- *You're here today for a reason, and that reason is...*

There is a caveat here. Make sure your opening line isn't just repeating your title slide. It should be something a little zestier. So, you wouldn't say, *"Today, I'm going to talk about communication skills."* Instead, you would say, *"Today, I'm going to teach you the single most important skill you can use to skyrocket your career..."*

Humor

Humor can be a great way to start because it boosts your likability and automatically makes people more open to your ideas. After all, it's harder to dislike someone who has just made you laugh. When it comes to humor, feel free to get creative. Try to think of an interesting or quirky one-liner about your topic, audience, or even yourself that will lighten the mood and set the stage for your content. I trust that you know what's appropriate for your audience!

A Question

The last optimal opener option is to ask a question that your audience would be curious about. This is another excellent way to instantly get their brains involved, creating interest and making sure they're ready to listen to you.

Here are a few options for how to phrase your opening question:

- *Have you ever thought about...?*
- *Did you know...?*
- *Do you ever wonder...?*

ENDING YOUR PRESENTATION

Just like you want to start with a boom, you'll want to end with a bang. People tend to remember the first and last things they heard the best, so let's look at the most effective ways to finish your presentation.

EASY SOLUTIONS

Keep the last few slides light on information. The information-heavy content should have already been covered. It's best if your final slides are persuasive and extremely easy to understand.

CLEAR CONCLUSIONS

Instead of ending with an awkward *"Sooo...does anyone have any questions?"* Have a designated closing slide. This slide can include a quick recap of your main idea or your call to action.

CALLS TO ACTION

When including a call to action, remember that human decisions are usually based on emotion first and then justified with logic later. So, when stating your CTA, make sure that you focus on the emotional advantages. You can start by highlighting the negative—what the future would look like if they don't take action. Then, you can move on to the positive, explaining how much better the future would look if your solution was implemented.

BONUSES

Everyone loves getting presents, especially when they don't expect one. So, at the end of your presentation, offer your listeners a little bonus gift to take with them. This could be a PDF with more information, interesting facts, relevant sources, or additional tips. Adding this extra "treat" works well for both in-person and virtual presentations.

PRACTICING YOUR PRESENTATION

Does your favorite actor roll up to set on shooting day without preparing and rehearsing beforehand? Of course not. While I'm not saying you need to be like Leonardo DiCaprio preparing for

The Revenant (apparently, he ate a lot of raw meat and slept in animal carcasses), the right type of practice will vastly improve your performance.

Experts recommend practicing in stages:

STAGE 1

Read through your entire presentation out loud as you go through your slides. How does it sound? Is your message clear? Make any necessary adjustments to ensure it sounds natural and has a good flow.

STAGE 2

Now that you're confident in your words, record yourself giving the presentation on video. Watch the video and take note of the other elements of communication—body language, facial expressions, hand gestures, and vocal tone.

Based on what you've learned so far in this book, how could you improve? Maybe you found yourself starting to slouch near the end. On the next practice round, you'll be conscious of maintaining a confident, upright posture throughout.

Maybe you thought your voice sounded monotone and your face was mostly expressionless. On the next run-through, you'll work on bringing more enthusiasm, varying your vocal tone, and smiling more.

There's also a chance you'll watch yourself and think, *"Wow, that was perfect! Not a single thing to improve on. I am the God of presenting!"*

If that's the case, I love your level of confidence! And because I like you so much, I must say that it's in your best interests to get a second opinion. It can be challenging to see your own faults, which is why working with a skilled (and honest) presenter is incredibly valuable.

Even the presentation specialist herself, Nancy Duarte, rehearsed with a speaking coach when preparing for her TED Talk. The feedback was invaluable because the coach pointed out things she would've never caught on her own.

Now, I understand there may not be a presentation expert in your life who can help you practice and provide quality feedback. Or maybe there is one, but you'd feel more comfortable working on your presentation with someone who doesn't know you personally.

If you'd like, you're welcome to reach out to me for advice on your next presentation. I've helped people from many different industries knock their presentations out of the park. If we end up working together, you can send me your slides, a video of yourself presenting, or we can set up a Zoom call to rehearse and provide live feedback.

Email ty@advancedgrowthinstitute.com by scanning the QR code below and we'll take it from there. I promise to get back to you within a couple of days.

Additionally, feel free to message me if you want to dive deeper into *any* of the other communication skills you've been learning about.

STAGE 3

In the final stage of preparation, it's time to do a full rehearsal. Your goal is to make this as close to the real thing as possible. Shower and get ready as if it's the day of the presentation, and put on the same clothes you will wear to present.

If it's in person, going to the same location to practice would be ideal, but this won't always be an option. That's okay—just do your best to recreate as many variables as you can. If you know you're going to be standing, practice standing. If it's virtual, make sure you have your lighting, camera angle, and background set up as if it's showtime.

Think of yourself as an elite athlete practicing for a playoff game. Or a famous actor getting ready to film a massive scene in their new movie. Or your favorite speaker preparing for their next big TED Talk. This is YOUR version of a playoff game. This is YOUR version of a new movie. This is YOUR version of a TED Talk. It's final preparation time. Let's go.

HOW TO RELAX BEFORE YOUR PRESENTATION

When it comes to calming your nerves and getting in the right state of mind before a presentation, you're already set up for success! The best techniques are the ones you've learned about in previous chapters. Remember, these techniques work exceptionally well before *any* stressful situation, whether it's an important presentation, meeting, job interview, or even a party (parties can be stressful for people too).

Let's review the best ways to relax before a presentation:

BOX BREATHING

1. Inhale slowly through your nose for 4 seconds
2. Hold your breath for 4 seconds
3. Exhale slowly (nose or mouth) for 4 seconds
4. Hold your breath for 4 seconds

On your inhales, allow your stomach to rise and expand as your lungs fill up with air. On your exhales, let your stomach fall as your abdomen muscles gently contract. Continue the full cycle of breathing until you feel focused and relaxed.

THE PHYSIOLOGICAL SIGH

1. Deep inhale through your nose
2. Add another inhale through your nose, but shorter this time
3. Extended exhale through your mouth

That's two consecutive inhales through the nose (one long, one short) followed by one long exhale through the mouth. The duration of your exhale should be longer than your two inhales. If you want, you can repeat it a second or third time, but typically one or two physiological sighs are all you need.

4-7-8 BREATHING

1. Inhale through your nose for 4 seconds
2. Hold your breath for 7 seconds
3. Exhale through your mouth for 8 seconds

When you're exhaling, close your lips into a small "o" shape, like you're blowing air through a straw, making a "whoosh" sound. Repeat the pattern three times for a total of four cycles.

SBVS—STRAIGHT, BREATHE, VISUALIZE, SMILE

1. Sit up straight with strong, confident posture
2. Take two physiological sighs
3. Visualize something that brings you joy
4. Smile

Just like video calls or meetings, if you need a little extra boost, you can add the bonus visualization here. Keep your eyes closed, and picture yourself going through the entire presentation. Imagine everything going perfectly. You're speaking clearly and confidently, everyone is deeply interested, and your audience absolutely loves you and your content.

Public speaking and presentations can be scary, but they can also feel incredibly rewarding, uplifting, and meaningful. When you know how to relax and calm your nerves, share ideas in a way that people find interesting, and connect with your audience, presentations can give you an amazing high. **If you follow the tips from this chapter, your presentations—along with your career—can skyrocket into the stratosphere of success.**

CHAPTER 10

FEEDBACK

" *Feedback is the breakfast of champions."*

—Ken Blanchard

S ince the beginning of time, feedback has been crucial to our survival. The feedback we received from eating berries taught us which ones could be eaten safely and which ones would poison and kill us. It taught us that certain plants could be smoked to chill out and feel mellow, and other plants would be toxic to our bodies if ingested.

Experimenting with different materials when building shelter and starting fires provided feedback on what worked and what didn't. This is how progress occurs—we try something out, get feedback on what happened, and then make adjustments to improve next time.

In our modern world, we are surrounded by feedback. Watches tell you how many calories you burned, rings tell you the quality of last night's sleep, and cars beep furiously at you for getting too close to another vehicle. Thanks to technology, we can constantly receive feedback on most aspects of our lives.

Technology may love to give us feedback, but getting consistent feedback in the business world seems to be lacking for many professionals. Because feedback is so important for career advancement, this is something we want to consciously take control of. **The accelerated growth from gaining and implementing feedback can lead to quicker promotions, expanded roles, and higher incomes.**

I'm a huge fan of self-evaluation, but if you never receive feedback from others, you could be flying blind and forced to guess what to work on next. You could be missing out on valuable insights on where to improve and how to make those improvements faster.

Despite the benefits of feedback, we are rarely taught how to successfully ask for it, receive it, or give it. That's what this chapter is for. Let's start with the first slice of the pie—*asking* for feedback.

HOW TO ASK FOR FEEDBACK

I dreaded feedback for many years when I entered the professional world. There was a lot of uncertainty and fear around what the other person might say, and I didn't want to risk feeling put down. My ego used to bruise like a peach, so I avoided feedback like a dog avoiding a vacuum.

Today, it's promising to see that most individuals already understand the value of feedback. The majority of professionals I work with are chomping at the bit to get more high-quality feedback, which is one of the main reasons I offer 1-on-1 coaching. They get real-time, powerful feedback every week. It's like putting your professional growth on steroids.

A PwC survey discovered that 60% of professionals want daily or weekly feedback, and it jumps to 72% for professionals under the age of 30 (Hogan, 2016). Furthermore, over **75% of professionals feel that they gain value from feedback, but *less than 30% actually receive it.***

With the exception of scheduled annual reviews, feedback can be a touchy topic that many choose to steer clear of. Why is this? Why don't we receive more of it?

It's likely one (or all) of these reasons:

- Your boss/leader was never taught the importance of feedback for their team members, so it's not something they often think about.
- They were never trained on how to *give* feedback, and they feel uncomfortable having these types of conversations.

- They're already busy enough, and they don't want to add more to their plate unless they think it's necessary.
- They're worried about saying something the "wrong" way and dealing with unpleasant emotional reactions.

Does that mean you should accept a life of minimal feedback? Far from it. All this means is that you can't rely on others to take initiative. You'll need to take charge and be proactive about getting your own feedback. You can't expect others to manage your success and be responsible for your development. You have more control than you think, and if you don't ask for feedback, you may not get what you need to perform at the highest level.

If you're feeling a bit uneasy about asking, you are far from alone. According to Ed Batista, Stanford Graduate School of Business instructor and executive coach, people tend to be hesitant to request feedback because of its stressful nature.

Fortunately, the more you do it, the easier it becomes—and the stronger *you* become. It's like hitting the gym for a lift or taking the stairs instead of the elevator each day. Batista says that if you're getting feedback regularly, there won't be as much to be surprised or stressed about, and there will be far more opportunities to make positive changes.

Sheila Heen, author of *Thanks for the Feedback: The Science and Art of Receiving Feedback Well*, says that **people who actively seek out negative feedback prove to be more satisfied.** These people aren't just looking to be praised; they honestly want to know what they're doing wrong and how they can improve.

Heen explains that these individuals receive superior performance reviews and adapt more easily and quickly to new positions, making them significantly more likely to be hired and promoted.

GETTING THE FEEDBACK YOU ACTUALLY NEED

So, how do you get feedback that is genuinely helpful? How do you get the kind of feedback that can be used to fast-track your growth?

Know What You Want

Start with yourself. Think about the type of feedback you'd like to receive first. Are you looking for general guidance on how to improve, or do you want your performance on a specific task or project to be evaluated? You'll be getting all kinds of feedback consistently from now on, so there's no wrong way to start; feel free to go with your gut. You'll need to decide this before speaking with your boss.

For this chapter, we will be talking about your boss as a main provider of feedback because of their direct impact on your career advancement, but you can use these tips with anyone you'd like advice from. I recommend seeking feedback from many different people. You'll want to ask those who are more successful than you or have already accomplished something you want to accomplish. The more information you get, the more you'll start to see patterns, and it will quickly become clear what you need to focus on.

Specific Questions

A common mistake when asking for feedback is asking comically vague questions. For example:

Person 1: *"Can you give me some feedback on that meeting?"*

Person 2: *"Sure, you did great."*

long pause

Person 1 (who wanted and expected more detail):
"Great. Thanks."

Person 2 (already checking their phone): *"No problem."*

Asking questions like this will rarely get you anything of value in return. **If you want specific answers, you have to ask specific questions.**

Asking *"What is one thing I could have done better in that meeting?"* would have got you a more specific answer. It also shows that you *actually want advice.* Sometimes, people ask questions like, *"How did I do?"* just because they want a little pat on the back. There's nothing wrong with that, but the back pat isn't our goal right now. We want to improve, and asking what you could have done better tells the other person exactly what you're looking for.

It's best to avoid questions that can be answered with a yes or a no. That brings us right back to our good friend from previous chapters—the open-ended question! An open-ended question starting with "how" or "what" will lead to more detailed responses. So, instead of *"Did that go well?"* ask questions such as:

- *How could I have been more convincing?*
- *How could I have a greater impact?*
- *What would you like to see less of?*
- *What would you like to see more of?*

If your manager says they'd like to see more of something from you, don't let them get away with being vague. Get them to go into detail on exactly *how* to do it. You want to walk away with clear actions to take. For example, if they say they'd like you to be more assertive, ask the following types of questions until you gain complete clarity on your next steps:

- *How would you recommend I be more assertive in the future?*
- *Can you give some examples of when I wasn't assertive enough?*
- *What can I do to show more assertiveness?*

Strategic Timing

If you want to get the best feedback possible, there's a time and a place to ask for it. Asking your boss about growth opportunities while they're in a bathroom stall might get you some weird answers. Popping in unexpectedly during their lunch is a risky move too. Hanger can be a very real and dangerously unpredictable thing for some people. By far, the best way to get feedback from your manager (or anyone else important) is to set up a meeting in advance.

ACTION STEP

Send an email to your boss asking to schedule your first feedback meeting. Here's a sample email you can use:

Good morning [Boss's Name],

I hope you had a great weekend.

*I've been thinking about my performance and would love
to get your feedback on how I can better serve you and
this organization.*

*Could we schedule a half-hour meeting to discuss your
thoughts on how I can improve?*

Any advice you can give is greatly appreciated.

Thank you,

[Your Name]

Once it's booked, prepare a list of questions based on our previous examples, and do your best to go in with an open mind. I'll explain more about best practices for receiving feedback shortly. After you finish your first feedback session, your goal is to make it a regular occurrence. Before you leave, say something like:

*"This was really valuable, and I appreciate you taking
the time to share your feedback. I'm confident that having these conversations regularly would help me progress
faster and contribute at a higher level. Are you open to a
half-hour feedback session every two weeks?"*

Chances are, your boss will be thrilled by your initiative to learn, your eagerness to improve, and your desire to help the company. Showing appreciation for their time and saying that you found their ideas valuable makes it even more likely you'll receive a positive response.

These meetings are one of the best ways to enhance your visibility in the workplace. Enhancing your visibility is tremendously powerful when it comes to advancing your career, and we'll go deep on it in the next chapter.

To make sure your boss is fully aware of your contributions, spend a few minutes at the beginning of these meetings giving them a brief update on the work you've been doing. You can ask, *"Would you mind if I give you a quick update on what I've been working on lately?"* This can be a natural transition into asking for feedback on particular projects.

Everything about this might sound extremely uncomfortable to you. A one-on-one meeting with your boss where they discuss things they don't like about you and your work? Who on earth would want to seek that out?

Well, asking for feedback the right way will help you receive constructive words and not just a bunch of *"I don't like when you _____ statements."* It might still feel incredibly awkward, but I promise it will pay enormous dividends for you and your career.

Ask Colleagues Too

Your leaders and mentors may give you the bulk of the advice, but you can also ask your colleagues for little bits of feedback. You don't have to schedule anything formal with your co-workers—it's okay to ask them more casually. Not casually in the bathroom, but casually after a meeting or while waiting for the elevator.

I bring up the bathroom again because a couple of years ago, I found myself inside the bathroom of a large organization. I had just finished giving their team a two-hour training session on communication in the workplace, and I was hydrated to the max.

As I'm peacefully doing my business, one of their younger executives suddenly bursts in and strolls right up to the urinal beside mine (for the record, there were three other urinals open.) He whips open his pants, looks right at me with a big grin on his face, and says, *"Great presentation! I know we just met, but what's the #1 thing I could do to improve my communication?"*

In his case, the #1 thing would be to ask for advice when his pants are fully on and he's not almost crossing streams with a stranger. Why do I tell this story? I tell this story in hopes of inspiring change. If this prevents even one awkward bathroom moment, the world will be a slightly better place.

HOW TO RECEIVE FEEDBACK

Now that you know feedback is an important ingredient in the recipe for professional development, and you know how to ask for it, how do you receive it without getting offended? How do you stay calm and open to receiving without getting defensive or emotional?

Whether it's from your boss, mentor, colleague, or even from anonymous surveys, being receptive to feedback is essential. But it's easier said than done. Our egos often get in the way of receptivity, and our instincts and emotions take over.

Our instincts classify negative feedback as a threat because it might lead to us being separated from the tribe. As we learned in previous chapters, our instincts think being separated from the tribe means reduced chances of survival.

When our brain senses this type of risk, it goes into fight-or-flight mode, increasing adrenaline and leading to a heightened emotional response. To overcome this, we need to shift our perspective away from viewing negative feedback as a threat. Consider it an opportunity for growth instead of a path to rejection and banishment from the group.

THE OPTIMIZED MINDSET FOR RECEIVING FEEDBACK

Viewing feedback with a growth mindset will make it a *lot* easier to receive. A growth mindset means you believe your skills and intelligence can be improved over time. So, even when you hear difficult feedback, you know you're capable of change and can overcome it. You're confident in your ability to learn, even if you're not good at it…yet.

Think of all feedback—even the negative kind—as a critical part of your professional success. It can help to imagine yourself as a castle. If you don't know your weak spots, opposing armies will keep invading, and you'll be helpless because you have no idea how they're getting in. When someone points out your areas of improvement, you know what you have to work on and can start acting accordingly. When you close those gaps and build up those weak spots, your castle becomes stronger and more powerful.

The learner's mindset from Chapter 1 absolutely loves feedback. Remember, the learner's identity is based on practice and progress, not achievement and results, so they welcome any opportunity to expand their horizons. The learner's sense of self is built on growth, and they relish all feedback because they know it will help them learn even faster.

RECEIVING FEEDBACK IN THE MOMENT

Resist Getting Defensive

Emotions can be challenging, so it's important you go into each feedback session calm, open-minded, and ready to listen. Take advantage of the breathing techniques you've learned (box breathing, 4-7-8 breathing, physiological sighs) or SBVS (sit up straight, breathe, visualize, smile) to make sure you're in the right headspace before receiving feedback.

If you get defensive and angry, or you start justifying your behavior and making excuses, people will likely avoid giving you honest feedback in the future. You could be missing out on valuable future advice from people if you respond aggressively, so it's important to stay cool as a cucumber.

If you're feeling overwhelmed at any point, it's best to mentally take a step back. Now would be a great time to use the physiological sigh—double inhale through the nose, long single exhale through the mouth. Remember, the science shows you only need one or two of these to feel calmer, and it can be done completely silently and discreetly without anyone noticing.

This is an excellent opportunity to practice controlling your emotions when you feel yourself getting worked up. **Being able to stay calm in stressful situations is a tremendously valuable skill to have in your career (and life).**

If you have to, you can be honest and tell the other person you need a little time to process their feedback and would prefer to move on. You can explore the feedback later in another meeting or address it over written communication as a last resort.

Active Listening

You'll get the most out of the interaction if you have your full attention on the speaker and actively listen to their comments. Instead of thinking of how you will respond to their remarks, use your brainpower to make sure you fully understand what they're saying. This is a perfect time to practice some of the active listening skills you learned earlier in the book—deep focus, paraphrasing their words back to them, using open-ended questions, and acknowledging their emotions as needed.

Additionally, maintain eye contact 60-70% of the time, keep your body language upright and open (no crossed arms), face your body toward the speaker, lean forward to demonstrate interest, show your hands, nod your head, and avoid fidgeting.

AFTER RECEIVING FEEDBACK

Maintain Perspective

First, keep in mind that if someone has given you feedback that you *really* don't resonate with, their views may not be universal. Everyone's perceptions are influenced by their individual values, beliefs, and life experiences. While the opinions of your bosses and mentors do matter, it can be helpful to recognize that each person interprets the words and actions of others through their own lens.

Verify It

To determine whether the feedback you received is simply one person's view, consider verifying with another trusted party. This doesn't mean hearing something negative from your boss and then running to your best work pal to ask, *"I don't do that, do I?"* It means seeking out other credible sources in an attempt to *validate* what you heard and then making a decision from there.

Make a Plan

When you receive feedback, it will always be your choice what to do with it. Certain things you'll want to jump on right away, some things you'll deposit in your memory bank for the time being, and other things you'll disregard entirely. While there's no obligation to change, all things being equal, **the more ideas you decide to take action on, the faster you will find yourself living the life you desire.**

No matter what category the feedback falls into, everything should be written down for you to refer back to. Look through your notes and decide what you will act on, then create a clear plan detailing how you will implement that feedback. If you're struggling to come up with a plan, ask for assistance from the person who gave you the feedback or anyone else you trust to give sound advice.

Finally, make notes in your calendar to evaluate your progress each week. When you feel like you've made notable changes, discuss with the feedback giver and get their thoughts on the work you've done so far. This will help keep you accountable and ensure you're putting in enough effort to see real improvements.

Accountability can be the missing piece that shoots you up to the next level of success. People often learn *how* to improve, but then they never spend enough time doing it to see any results. There's a reason why coaching is a multi-billion dollar industry.

Some individuals can excel on their own, but many people need consistent accountability and expert guidance in order to make progress at the speed they desire. When you have a professional holding you accountable, and you invest in yourself, you show up in a much different way—and that's when you get real, life-changing results.

I never planned on coaching individuals when I first started in this space, but after seeing how a person's life can transform with a little extra help, it's now one of the most rewarding parts of my business. I've seen people land their dream jobs, score huge promotions, double their incomes, find loving partners, fix their relationships, make lifelong friends, and so much more.

All I did was give them the right tools, offer guidance and support, and keep them on track when things got tough. That's what I love about communication skills. They can be used to improve almost every aspect of your life, and once you have them, you get to enjoy their benefits for the rest of time.

If you're interested in learning more about coaching, visit www.advancedgrowthinstitute.com/coaching by scanning the QR code below:

You can also email me at ty@advancedgrowthinstitute.com, or book a free video call with me at www.calendly.com/ty-hoesgen. All you have to do is scan the QR code below, select the individual option, and pick a time that works best for you.

If it wasn't obvious, I love QR codes. They're remarkably efficient. Even if you only save a few seconds of typing, optimizing a process is so satisfying.

HOW TO GIVE FEEDBACK

When it comes to feedback early in your career, learning how to *ask for* and *receive it* will be the most valuable to your knowledge-hungry self. That being said, knowing how to *give* feedback is also an important skill to keep in mind.

Even if you're not giving much feedback yet, you never know when an influential person might ask for your opinion, and having the ability to provide high-quality feedback can make you stand out. No matter what, as you advance in your career, there will come a time when you're suddenly expected to give it on a regular basis.

Because we are rarely taught how to give feedback, if someone asks for it, many of us give responses that are unclear and not actionable. I used to be the worst for this.

"I thought it was great—very helpful!" or *"Not too bad...definitely some interesting points in there."* These used to be my go-to responses if someone asked for my input. I'd use the first one if I liked whatever they were asking about (meeting, report, etc.) and the second one if I didn't like it. Unsurprisingly, I don't think this advice had much of an impact.

If feedback isn't actionable, it's a waste of time. It's like telling someone, *"You're too tall"* or *"You're too short."* They can't change their height, so this feedback is pointless. **If you want to provide genuinely useful feedback, always include three main components—behavior, outcome, and future action.**

For **behavior**, be sure to address specific things that a person did. Provide clear examples of behavior you want them to repeat or avoid, focusing on the behaviors themselves instead of the person's character.

Next, include the **outcome** of the behavior in question. Explain how the behavior affects them, others, or the organization. Finally, provide them with specific **future actions** to take. These are the action steps that will help facilitate their growth.

For example:

> *"During yesterday's presentation, you seemed to ramble a bit after making your point* (behavior), *and it looked like the client was starting to zone out* (outcome). *You gave too many details* (behavior), *and they*

seemed a little confused (outcome). *When we talk informally, you know the topic well and get to the point quickly, so I'm confident this will be an easy fix for your presentations. Next time, let's do a couple of trial runs together to make sure everything is clear and concise before meeting with the client* (future action).

GENERAL TIPS FOR GIVING FEEDBACK

- Make it about their behavior, not about the person
- Frame it from *your* perspective
- Be as specific as possible
- Give concrete examples of behavior
- Explain the outcomes of said behavior
- Provide future action steps to help them improve
- Always include *some* positive feedback
- Connect your feedback to their long-term goals
- To reduce the chances of misinterpretation, provide feedback in person whenever possible. (If face-to-face isn't feasible, video calls are your next best option.)

Feedback is an often-overlooked piece of the puzzle when it comes to advancing your career, but if used correctly, it's one of the most powerful ways to speed up your progress. Seek feedback from your bosses, co-workers, and any mentors you have in your life.

The more feedback you get, the more you'll start to see patterns, and the easier it will be to choose the best ways to spend your time and energy. The accelerated growth that comes from implementing quality feedback can lead to faster promotions, expanded roles, and higher incomes.

CHAPTER 11

VISIBILITY

> ❝ *To be vulnerable—to really put yourself out there, and lean into it—is to live courageously."*
>
> **—Brene Brown**

You've been working hard. You've been reading and reviewing this book and diligently practicing your communication skills. You've been putting in that work! You've made a ton of improvements and have noticed positive changes. You feel and look more confident, people seem to respect and listen to you more, and your interactions are flowing far easier than ever before. Despite all of your improvements, it doesn't feel like you're getting any more recognition from your bosses. What could the cause of this be?

There's an excellent chance it's the same reason that many great employees get overlooked for raises and promotions—a lack of visibility.

Some people are naturals when it comes to marketing themselves. They're great at showing off their accomplishments and making their value known to the high-level executives in the organization. Some take this a little too far and cross the line into arrogant territory, which annoys and alienates most of the people around them. Others need a little push in the right direction to get themselves noticed and receive the recognition and opportunities they deserve.

If you're part of the last group, this chapter is for you.

HOP OUT OF THE BUSHES

When I talk to professionals about visibility, they'll occasionally say things like, *"I like to fly under the radar. I prefer to keep my head down and just do my work. I work hard, and that's what matters."*

While hard work is undoubtedly a critical factor for professional success, you need to think beyond working hard if you want to rapidly advance your career. It's time to consider your visibility in the workplace.

Do the people that can move your career forward know how hard you work? If you like to *"fly under the radar,"* chances are, they don't know it well enough. You might think your bosses know everything you're doing, but that's unlikely. The people in managerial positions have many moving parts to deal with, so they usually can't (or won't) keep track of what every employee is doing. As a result, they don't always see the full value each individual provides. This is especially true in big companies, but also in small ones—managers usually have too much on their own plate to keep track of everything on yours.

If your motto is to keep your head down and forge ahead, you'll end up missing out on great opportunities, no matter how hard you work. Whether it's fair or not, this is the reality of the world. The people who can help advance your career need to be able to see the full impact of what you're doing and the total value you're bringing.

So, what does this mean for you? It means that if you want to get ahead and reach your peak potential, then you're going to have to hop out of the metaphorical bushes. Unless you're a sniper or a spy, hiding in the bushes is not part of your job description.

In other words, it's time to gain proper visibility in the workplace. We're going to make sure that the right people know about your skills, expertise, and accomplishments, and that everyone knows how valuable you are to the organization. That way, when it comes time for a raise or promotion, you're the first one on their mind.

Another statement I hear from clients when talking about their visibility is some version of, *"There's already enough loud personalities in this organization. I don't want to talk about myself and be annoying like them."*

Fortunately, the goal is to get seen in a positive way, not annoy everyone around you. You don't have to go around boisterously bragging to increase your visibility at work, and there's a big difference between boasting and demonstrating your value. You can build your visibility and credibility in a way that is both doable and comfortable for you, no matter how shy or humble you are.

While humility is a good thing, humility to the point of invisibility is not. You have to ensure that all the hard work you put in doesn't fade into the background. It's important that others are aware of what you do and why it's essential to the company.

Let's look at how to maximize your visibility and make your value known without sounding like a cheesy infomercial.

SHARE WHAT YOU LEARNED

If you were asked to analyze your competitors and write a report on your findings, it would be a bit silly to go around telling everybody that you completed the task. It's part of your job, after all. But simply emailing the report to your boss, checking off the box on your to-do list, and calling it a day isn't enough to increase your visibility.

So, what can you do? First, you'll want to share anything of value with the people in your organization. Share information that you know others would benefit from knowing.

In this example, you might have learned that one of your main competitors just introduced a new line of business or formed a new partnership. You could share the key points from your analysis at the next team meeting. Alternatively, you could send an email to the team summarizing your findings, making sure you include anyone on the leadership team that might find value in this information. Use the tips you learned in the written communication chapter to keep your message short, easy to read, and focused on the recipient.

PRESENT YOUR OWN WORK

Let's say your boss asks you to create a report that you know will be presented to upper management. Usually, you would prepare the report and hand it over, secretly grateful that you don't have to stand up and talk about it yourself.

This is certainly the easiest route, but it's not the most effective way to climb the corporate ladder. So, ask your boss if they would be comfortable with you presenting the information yourself. If your boss is anything like me and the many leaders I've worked with, they will love your initiative. At the very least, they may still want to lead the discussion but will gladly involve you in the meeting. After you sit in on a few of these meetings, there's a strong chance you'll eventually be given the opportunity to speak.

If you never present your own findings, there's a risk that the higher-ups will always think your boss is doing this work instead of you. That's not to say your boss is trying to steal your work; it's more likely they are so focused on getting things done that the idea of attributing the work doesn't even cross their mind.

You want the influential people in your organization to be aware of the significant work you're doing, and presenting your work in these situations is one of the most effective ways to accomplish this.

PRACTICE STRATEGIC GRATITUDE

Another way to gain more visibility is by connecting directly with the key executives in your organization. Send them a message showing your appreciation for something they did or said. Reveal how it affected you, how you applied the advice, and what came of it.

Most people never do this because they think the executives are too busy to be bothered. While they are busy, they also have the highest expectations placed on them, so they tend to get very few "Thank you" messages. That means sending a genuine note of appreciation will be more meaningful to them, making your message (and you) stand out.

There's a right and wrong way to do this. Sending a vague "You're great" message without any information will just seem self-serving and irritating. Instead, provide clear and specific details about how their words or actions helped you improve or accomplish something.

REQUEST GUIDANCE

There's absolutely nothing wrong with asking for help. In fact, it's a great way to make a genuine and productive connection with leaders in your organization.

In the last chapter on feedback, you learned about having regular meetings with your boss to discuss opportunities for improvement. These check-ins will go a long way—not only increasing your visibility to *that* manager—but also to other upper-level executives in the company.

As your relationship with your manager develops, they will start praising your dedication to growth and talking to other executives about how much you care about your work. Your performance reflects positively on them, so it's in their best interests to speak highly of you. This is why consistent communication with your boss is so important—they can't talk you up to others if they don't hear about your progress.

It doesn't have to be as often, but you can have these feedback conversations with other influential people as well. Send a short message to a leader you want to connect with and ask for 15 minutes of their time to get their advice on an idea or project you're working on. Especially when you make it clear you aren't looking to take an hour of their day, most people will gladly accept your request. People love to feel knowledgeable, important, and valued, and that's how they feel anytime you ask for their advice. Asking someone for advice is one of the best ways to make a person like you.

LOOK BEYOND YOUR DEPARTMENT

Many of us shy types like to stay in our bubbles, and we tend to avoid branching off to meet new people. At work, we'll sometimes create imaginary barriers and interact with other departments as little as possible. After all, it feels safer and more comfortable to stay within our team because we know everyone.

This is another situation where the comfortable route isn't the best one for long-term success. By building relationships with different people across various departments in your organization, you improve your chances of succeeding professionally. The more connections you have, the more people there are to help you, support you, and recommend you for new opportunities. Plus, you never know whose uncle could end up being the CEO of the company of your dreams.

I want to stress that it's important to be sincere. Your goal should be to have a positive impact on others and form genuine friendships. While this may be one of the fastest, most powerful ways to advance your career, it's also a wonderful way to make your life more fulfilling and enjoyable.

STEP UP TO THE PLATE

There are always certain issues in an organization that people love to avoid. You know, like the product that keeps getting passed around because its performance has been lackluster forever. Everyone wants to work on the new, exciting products or handle the areas that generally do a lot of business.

If you step up to the plate and volunteer to take on the problems everyone else avoids, you will immediately set yourself apart. Even if you don't have massive success in turning the situation around, you'll still get credit for being bold and rising to the challenge.

And if you do have some success, it's like getting double bonus points for your reputation. You'll start being known as someone who isn't afraid to get their hands dirty and tackle difficult tasks. People with this trait are highly valued in any organization and are one of the first to be put forward for promotions.

TECH DIRTY TO ME

Another way to increase your visibility in the workplace is to analyze what your organization currently does and find areas for improvement. One area where this works especially well is technology, and you don't need to be a tech expert to make an impact.

For example, let's say that in your previous organization, you used a customer relationship management (CRM) software that made it incredibly easy to organize and manage all of your clients. Now, in your new role, you discover the company you're working for is still using slow and outdated in-house software. This is a perfect opportunity for you to speak about the advantages of your previous CRM and encourage your company to consider an upgraded solution. Remember to use the PREP framework to explain your point!

Not only will the software benefit the organization, but when you bring this up, it shows that you care about the company's performance and are willing to dedicate time and effort to find ways to improve it.

VOLUNTEER YOUR TIME

You can also gain more visibility by volunteering your time. You know those committees, conferences, and events that many people avoid like the plague? You don't need to attend *all* of them (I could never ask that of you. I like you, after all), but it's strongly recommended that you start getting involved with *some* of them.

Participating in anything that requires you to interact outside your regular contacts list is a great way to expand your network. These are opportunities to get in front of many different individuals that you'd normally never get the chance to spend time with. When you're meeting people in these situations, it's always a good idea to mention what you do for work and offer to help in any way you can.

Just like forming friendships outside of your circle, when you offer to give your time, there's no hidden agenda and no expectations of receiving anything in return. I've found that anytime I give to others this way, whether it's time, money, or energy, I always end up getting rewarded in return. And damn, does giving to other people ever feel good.

When I first started teaching piano lessons as a side hustle, I struggled to get clients. One night, while staying up late reading an article about *"The Top Ways to Ask Great Questions,"* I came across an ad for a volunteer piano teacher position.

The position was part of a program created for underprivileged children. Music teachers would volunteer their time teaching kids whose parents couldn't afford lessons. What a wonderfully heart-warming idea, I thought! I responded to the ad, and after a quick interview and criminal record check, I was in.

I was amazed at how fast some of the kids were able to learn. It was truly remarkable watching their tiny brains absorb everything and seeing their progress week by week. I posted an Instagram story talking about how awesome these little humans were, and an old friend replied to the story asking if I'd be willing to teach his son. Then, someone from the gym replied, asking about lessons for their daughter. My phone started blowing up. I ended up gaining more students in one day than I had in the past two months, without even trying. What's the lesson here? I believe if you give your time with pure intentions, focus on helping others, and aim to make the world a better place, you will be rewarded.

KNOWLEDGE ACQUISITION

Many companies have "education dollars," which is money budgeted specifically for their employees to upgrade their knowledge and skills. These dollars are often used for seminars, courses, lunch-and-learns, etc. If your company already offers education sessions from experts outside of your organization, make sure you take advantage and use them as a way to increase your visibility.

Active participation in these sessions is an excellent way to do this. Ask questions, take notes, and share your thoughts when the speaker asks for input. Trust me—as a boss, there's nothing worse than paying an expert to come in and educate your staff, only to watch them sit there and not engage. On the flip side, there's nothing better than seeing your team focused and showing a genuine interest in learning. It's like seeing a child walk for the first time.

Anytime you have one of these seminars, it's an opportunity to solidify yourself as someone with a thirst for knowledge and a strong desire to improve. I can't emphasize enough how highly you will be viewed by the leadership team if this is the reputation you build for yourself.

If you never have education sessions at your workplace, you can make a name for yourself by pitching the idea to your manager. Tell your boss you're looking to accelerate your growth and gain new information to serve the company better. Ask if they've ever considered bringing in professionals from outside the organization to teach the team new skills. It helps if you already have a type of speaker in mind and how the content will assist you and your team.

For example, organizations hire me to train their teams on how to improve their communication skills, and they can choose the theme of each training based on what's best suited for them.

Some of the most popular themes are:

- Enhancing connections with clients to boost sales
- Maximizing customer satisfaction and retention
- The power of active listening and asking the right questions
- Building harmony—helping teams connect and get along peacefully

If you don't know where to begin with this type of education, you can have my team and I do all of the work for you. To get the process started, you can choose one of two options:

1. **Email me at ty@advancedgrowthinstitute.com (just scan the QR code below) and say, "*Hey Ty, can you water my team's brains with more knowledge?*"**

I promise to respond within a couple of days. If it takes longer, please email our Support Team: support@advancedgrowthinstitute.com

2. You can also book a free video call with me at www. calendly.com/ty-hoesgen to discuss how I can help your team. All you have to do is scan the QR code below, select the corporate option, and pick a time that works best for you.

You're welcome to have your boss (or whoever is responsible for education in your organization) reach out as well. Once we've locked down a date, I'll deposit a *big, juicy referral bonus* into your bank account.

ACTION STEP

Now that we've covered nine powerful ways to increase your visibility at work, pick two ways that resonate with you the most and start incorporating them over the next two weeks. After that, you can keep adding one per week until your visibility skyrockets, and it becomes abundantly clear to everyone how valuable you are to the organization. **When you have elite communication skills combined with peak visibility, you're in the best possible position for raises, promotions, and new growth opportunities, and you're ready to rapidly advance your career.**

A FAVOR TO ASK

If you recall from earlier in the book, the secret to living a happier, healthier, and wealthier life is **the simple act of helping others.**

People who help others get to:

- Enjoy higher levels of happiness
- Make more money
- Live longer, more meaningful lives

With that being said, could I ask you for a favor?

The only way for our team at Advanced Growth Institute to help as many people as possible is, first, by reaching them. And while I love the quote, *"Don't judge a book by its cover,"* many people do, in fact, judge books by their covers—and their reviews.

If you found this book valuable in any way, would you please take a moment right now and leave an honest review of the book? **It will cost you $0 and less than 60 seconds.**

Your review will help:

- One more awkward person feel more confident.
- One more high achiever unlock their skills.
- One more professional advance their career.
- One more person live the life of their dreams.

To help your fellow humans, all you have to do is—and it takes less than 60 seconds—leave a review.

Would you please scan the QR code below and submit a quick review before moving on? This takes you right to the review page:

You, my friend—you are the best! This is why I'm your biggest fan. Thank you.

" *You will either step forward into growth, or you will step back into safety."*

—Abraham Maslow

If you're anything like the vast majority of people in the world, when you started reading this book, you were being held back—either consciously, unconsciously, or both—by a set of limitations you'd put on yourself or others had placed upon you.

Maybe you were looking for that next big promotion and raise, but your inner voice kept telling you that you weren't good enough. Maybe you wanted to quit your job and explore a new career path, but a part of you kept holding you back. Maybe you wanted to boost your confidence, get more respect, and finally be taken seriously, but it seemed almost impossible given where you're at right now. Maybe you were convinced that you would always be stuck, and you'd never step into your power and live up to your potential.

If you've ever felt like this in any way, now that you've finished this book, it's time to say goodbye to that previous version of you. It's time to release your past self—their uncertainties, fears, and limiting beliefs—and say hello to the new you. **The new you is a grower. The new you is a learner. The new you is limitless.**

You no longer allow yourself to be held back. There may be a lot of things you haven't done yet, and there may be things you've struggled with in the past, but you know your past doesn't create your future. You, right now, in this very moment—you are the one that creates your future. You know you're capable of anything you set your mind to, and **you are more powerful than you could ever imagine.**

I believe everything happens for a reason. I'm not sure what initially drew you to this book or how you ended up with it, but I don't think it was a coincidence. Even if it doesn't seem like it yet, this could be a sign that you're about to begin a new chapter in your life. A chapter of tremendous growth and significant transformation.

In your hands, you have access to all the tools needed to master your communication skills and make this next stage of your life an extraordinary one.

You know how to set yourself up for success by approaching your journey with the learner's mindset. You only compare yourself to yesterday's you, and you understand the power of the word "yet." (Chapter 1)

You know how to use powerful posture, eye contact, and hand gestures to look and feel confident, energetic, and influential. (Chapter 2)

You know the best practices for speaking up in meetings and how to clearly explain your thoughts and ideas. (Chapter 3)

You know how to use active listening to make people feel heard, understood, and valued, and you get to enjoy the added bonus of enhanced learning and memory. (Chapter 4)

You understand nonverbal cues and know how to read them—giving you remarkable insight into what people are *really* thinking and feeling. (Chapter 5)

You know how to optimize your voice, use mirroring to increase connection, and make your phone calls smooth and successful. (Chapter 6)

You know how to write in an effective, reader-friendly way that makes people feel good about responding to you and taking action. (Chapter 7)

You know how to look and sound like a true professional on video calls, and you avoid the common virtual mistakes that many people make. (Chapter 8)

You know how to wow your audience with engaging, memorable presentations, and you know the top techniques to relax and optimize your state of mind before a presentation (or any other stressful situation). (Chapter 9)

You recognize the value of feedback for your growth and development, and you know how to properly ask for it, receive it, and give it. (Chapter 10)

You understand how important visibility is for your career advancement, and you know multiple ways to increase it and boost your success. (Chapter 11)

If you haven't yet, it's time to start using what you've learned in your everyday life. You'll definitely want to use these tips when you're at work, and you'll make progress even faster if you use them at home, out with your friends, or when you're running errands. Skills like body language, listening, reading nonverbal cues, and mirroring can be practiced any time you interact with another person.

You can choose which skills you want to work on first, but the most important thing is that you start *somewhere*. Anywhere. And when you do, I think you'll be amazed at who you can become.

If you're still questioning yourself, the fact that you read this book from start to finish is proof that you're serious about taking your life to the next level. You could have spent this time doing any number of things, and you chose to work on yourself.

Not only that, but you chose to learn about skills that most people never even think about. I'm proud of you! If I could reach through this page and give you a fist bump, I would. In fact, I'm optimistic we'll be able to do that in the 2030 revised version.

As you build your elite communication skills, you'll have more control over your life than ever before. You'll find yourself getting more respect from everyone you meet. People will admire and look up to you in ways you never thought possible. Every interaction you have will become significantly easier. You'll be better equipped to help others and offer your unique value to the world. You'll be in the best possible position to thrive in your career, relationships, and all areas of life.

As these communication skills become rooted inside of your ever-growing brain, you will be able to apply them in any situation that involves other people—personally and professionally—and you'll be able to use them to your advantage for the rest of time. While you evolve, I only ask one thing…that you use your powers for good.

To your growth,

Ty Hoesgen
Founder, Advanced Growth Institute

P.S. I appreciate you. I appreciate you for taking the time to read this book, and I appreciate your dedication to self-improvement. You are my favorite type of person, and it was a pleasure writing this book for you. If you enjoyed *Elite Communication Skills for Young Professionals*, please share it with others. Gift it to a friend, loan it to a co-worker, or give it to someone who could use a boost. You could also buy 100 copies and be like Oprah: *"You get a book, and you get a book, and you get a book! Everyone gets a book!"* Whatever you choose to do, thank you.

HOW CAN TY HELP YOU?

CORPORATE

Corporate Speaking Engagements—for teams who recognize the value of communication.

Ty teaches attendees powerful, science-backed communication strategies that anyone can apply to enjoy more success at work.

He shares verbal and nonverbal tools for strengthening professional relationships, building trust and influence, and connecting better with co-workers, leaders, clients, and customers.

Depending on your organization's goals, Ty can tailor the presentation to what your team needs most.

Here are some of the most popular themes:

- Enhancing connections with your clients to boost sales
- Maximizing customer satisfaction and retention
- The power of active listening and asking the right questions
- Building harmony in the workplace—helping teams connect and get along peacefully

If you'd like to book Ty to speak to your team—or if you have any questions—please email ty@advancedgrowthinstitute.com by scanning the QR code below:

You can also book a free video call with Ty at www.calendly. com/ty-hoesgen to discuss how he can help your team. All you have to do is scan the QR code below, select the corporate option, and pick a time that works best for you.

HOW CAN TY HELP YOU?

INDIVIDUAL

Private Coaching and Mentoring—for individuals looking to gain a positively unfair advantage in their life and career...faster.

If you're anything like Ty used to be, you often watch videos or read books and have the best *intentions* of implementing what you learned, but after a while, you end up going back to your usual habits…and not much changes.

If this ever happens to you, it doesn't have to keep being that way. Imagine the changes you would see in your life if you started taking more strategic action. Would you be further ahead in your career? Would you be making more money? Would you have better relationships?

Allow yourself to imagine what that evolved version of you looks like. Imagine yourself as that highly successful and confident professional everyone admires and looks up to.

That version of you exists—it just needs to be unlocked. That's why having a dedicated coach and program is so valuable.

When you have a professional guiding you step by step and holding you accountable, that's when you show up as your best self…and that's when you get to experience real, life-changing results much faster.

We know you're super busy, so we created the *Powerful People Skills Program,* where you only have to commit to **1 hour per week.**

Because you're already interacting with people at work daily, even if you work from home, there are plenty of opportunities to optimize your skills, so you don't even have to set aside additional time.

No matter where you're at with your people skills right now, Ty will work with you to make sure you achieve the changes you want in your life.

And to help ease your mind, he added multiple guarantees and set everything up so there is <u>zero risk for you.</u>

If you want to level up your life *(without having to make crazy sacrifices or be inauthentic),* **visit www.advancedgrowthinstitute.com/coaching by scanning the QR code below:**

You can also email ty@advancedgrowthinstitute.com, or book a free video call with him at www.calendly.com/ty-hoesgen. All you have to do is scan the QR code below, select the individual option, and pick a time that works best for you.

YOUR FREE GIFT

THE INSTANT LIKABILITY ONLINE COURSE

*How to Be Instantly Likable to Fast-Track Your Success
(While Still Being Your Authentic Self)*

Research has revealed that, in addition to communication, **likability
is actually more important than competence when it comes to
being successful.**

Studies have shown that the more likable a person is, the more likely
they are to <u>get promotions, pay increases, and see faster career jumps.</u>

If you improve your likability, everything you do with communication will automatically become easier.

In our *Instant Likability* course, you will discover:

➜ 5 phrases that make you instantly more likable
➜ The shockingly easy likability strategy anyone can use
➜ The #1 word you should avoid at all costs

If you're interested in watching, I set up a page at www.instant-likability.com/free-access (QR code below) that allows readers of
Elite Communication Skills for Young Professionals to **skip the $97 pay-
ment step.**

I'd like to give it to you as a gift of appreciation for reading this book. Your support really means a lot to me.

—Your biggest fan, Ty Hoesgen
Founder, Advanced Growth Institute

Ty Hoesgen is the Founder of Advanced Growth Institute and the author of *Elite Communication Skills for Young Professionals.* He is a writer, speaker, consultant, and coach who specializes in (and is slightly obsessed with) communication and people skills.

Motivated by his past struggles, Ty has spent many years and thousands of hours researching, practicing, and experimenting in order to master the world of communication.

Determined to make others' journeys less painful than his own, he focuses on creating practical, entertaining resources that make growth and transformation quicker, easier, and more enjoyable.

His life is currently dedicated to helping individuals and organizations around the world reach their peak potential by improving their communication skills.

Ty lives happily with his wonderfully communicative partner Liza in downtown Toronto. To this day, he firmly believes he would have never scored an extraordinary woman like Liza if he hadn't worked so hard on his communication.

When he isn't working, Ty enjoys lifting weights, playing piano, experimenting with breathwork, and seeing how long he can last in saunas and ice baths.

20 Astonishing Video Conferencing Statistics for 2021. (2021, July 10). *Digital in the Round*. https://digitalintheround.com/video-conferencing-statistics/

60 Hand Gestures You Should Be Using and Their Meaning. (2021, March 16). Science of People. https://www.scienceofpeople.com/hand-gestures/

7 Benefits of a Standing Desk. (2017, June 18). Healthline. https://www.healthline.com/nutrition/7-benefits-of-a-standing-desk

Adobe Workfront. (2021). *State of Work 2021 | Adobe Workfront*. https://www.workfront.com/campaigns/state-of-work

Allan Pease. (2013, November 17). *Body language, the power is in the palm of your hands | Allan Pease | TEDxMacquarieUniversity*. https://www.youtube.com/watch?v=ZZZ7k8cMA-4

Amazing Presentations. (2014, April 25). Duarte. https://www.duarte.com/amazing-presentations-structure-your-presentation-like-a-story/

Andrade, J. (2010). What does doodling do? *Applied Cognitive Psychology, 24*(1), 100–106. https://doi.org/10.1002/acp.1561

Arora, A. (2021, June 23). *7 Ways Effective Presentations are Helpful in Your Career Advancement*. Business 2 Community. https://www.business2community.com/communications/7-ways-effective-presentations-are-helpful-in-your-career-advancement-02415305

Azzarello, P. (2014, June 5). *The Very Real Problems When You Decide to Fly Under the Radar.* TLNT. https://www.tlnt.com/the-very-real-problems-when-you-decide-to-fly-under-the-radar/

Bahns, A. J., Crandall, C. S., Gillath, O., & Preacher, K. J. (2017). Similarity in relationships as niche construction: Choice, stability, and influence within dyads in a free choice environment. *Journal of Personality and Social Psychology, 112*(2), 329–355. https://doi.org/10.1037/pspp0000088

Bajic, E. (2015, July 28). *7 Ways To Raise Your Visibility And Advance Your Career.* Forbes. https://www.forbes.com/sites/elenabajic/2015/07/28/7-ways-to-raise-your-visibility-and-advance-your-career/

Barnard, D. (2021, March 3). *How to Develop Effective Verbal Communication Skills.* Virtual Speech. https://virtualspeech.com/blog/verbal-communication-skills

Bartlett, L. (2019, October 22). *How Your Smile Affects Your Self-Esteem.* House of Coco. https://houseofcoco.net/how-your-smile-affects-your-self-esteem/

Bell, M. (2020, December 9). *3 Breathing Techniques That Relieve Stress and Strengthen Your Lungs.* The Health Science Journal. https://www.thehealthsciencejournal.com/3-breathing-techniques-that-relieve-stress-and-strengthen-your-lungs/

Beohm, R. (2018, June 27). What To Do When You See Negative Body Language | Rachel Beohm. *Rachel Beohm.* https://www.rachelbeohm.com/what-to-do-when-you-see-negative-body-language/

Besieux, T., Edmondson, A. C., & Vries, F. de. (2021, June 11). How to Overcome Your Fear of Speaking Up in Meetings. *Harvard Business Review.* https://hbr.org/2021/06/how-to-overcome-your-fear-of-speaking-up-in-meetings

Bilyeu, T. (2017, July 24). 3 Mental Upgrades That Will Propel You to Achievement. *Impact Theory.* https://impacttheory.com/blog/3-mental-upgrades-will-propel-achievement/

Bloom. (2019, December 17). *Visual Communication: 6 Tips for Creating Captivating Visuals &ndash.* Bloom Communications. https://bloomcommunications.com/visual-communication-6-tips-for-creating-captivating-visuals/

Body Language In The Workplace: 15 Cues You Must Know. (2014, November 7). Science of People. https://www.scienceofpeople.com/office-body-language/

Boogaard, K. (2018, November 15). *Why speaking up at work is important and how to do it.* Work Life by Atlassian. https://www.atlassian.com/blog/confluence/speaking-up-at-work

Boogard, K. (2017, October 17). *4 Ways To Make Your Painfully Long Email Shorter.* Fast Company. https://www.fastcompany.com/40481644/4-ways-to-make-your-painfully-long-email-shorter

Bradford, W. C. (2004). Reaching the visual learner: teaching property through art. *The Law Teacher, Vol. 11(2004).* https://ssrn.com/abstract=587201

Branson, R. (2015, November 5). *My top 10 quotes on communication | Virgin.* Virgin.Com. https://virgin.com/branson-family/richard-branson-blog/my-top-10-quotes-communication

Brennan, D. (2021, June 9). *What to Know About 4-7-8 Breathing*. WebMD. https://www.webmd.com/balance/what-to-know-4-7-8-breathing

Broaders, S. C., Cook, S. W., Mitchell, Z., & Goldin-Meadow, S. (2007). Making children gesture brings out implicit knowledge and leads to learning. *Journal of Experimental Psychology. General, 136*(4), 539–550. https://doi.org/10.1037/0096-3445.136.4.539

Brownlee, D. (2020, June 8). *Are You Really Listening Or Just Waiting To Talk? There's A Difference*. Forbes. https://www.forbes.com/sites/danabrownlee/2020/08/06/are-you-really-listening-or-just-waiting-to-talk-theres-a-difference/

Brunson, R. (2017). *Expert Secrets: The Underground Playbook for Creating a Mass Movement of People Who Will Pay for Your Advice*. Morgan James Publishing

Building Confidence and Conquering the Fear of Speaking Up. (2021, February 1). *IAWomen Blog*. https://blog.iawomen.com/building-confidence-and-the-conquering-the-fear-of-speaking-up/

Cain, S. (2013). *Quiet: The power of introverts in a world that can't stop talking* (1st pbk. ed). Broadway Paperbacks.

Campolo, Esq., J. (2021, April 20). *Take Control of Your Negotiation Using Active Listening Techniques*. Campolo, Middleton & McCormick, LLP. https://cmmllp.com/take-control-of-your-negotiation-using-active-listening-techniques/

Chin, A. (2015, March 9). With body language, the power is in the palm of your hands. *Resource Media*. https://www.resource-media.org/body-language-the-power-is-in-the-palm-of-your-hands/

Cho, W. (2019, February 12). *Compare Yourself To Who You Were Yesterday*. Medium. https://mystudentvoices.com/compare-yourself-to-who-you-were-yesterday-5bb9d4f31b8f

Communication Skills: How to Use Active Listening and Open Ended Questions. (2011, April 28). Knoji. https://knoji.com/article/communication-skills-how-to-use-active-listening-and-open-ended-questions/

Contrast In Presentations Creates Contour. (2014, June 30). Duarte. https://www.duarte.com/contrast-in-presentations-creates-contour/

Cook, S. W., Yip, T. K., & Goldin-Meadow, S. (2010). Gesturing makes memories that last. *Journal of Memory and Language*, *63*(4), 465–475. https://doi.org/10.1016/j.jml.2010.07.002

Cooper, B. B. (2013, August 8). *5 Habits of Highly Effective Communicators*. Buffer Resources. https://buffer.com/resources/why-talking-about-ourselves-is-as-rewarding-as-sex-the-science-of-conversations/

Coren, M. J. (2016, June 10). *Too many workers aren't wearing pants on video calls*. Quartz. https://qz.com/703513/too-many-workers-arent-wearing-pants-on-video-calls/

Council, F. C. (2019, June 18). *11 Nonverbal Cues Every Professional Should Learn To Read*. Forbes. https://www.forbes.com/

sites/forbescoachescouncil/2019/06/18/11-nonverbal-cues-every-professional-should-learn-to-read/

Council, F. C. (2020, July 17). *13 Times In-Person Communication Is Better Than Electronic Exchanges.* Forbes. https://www.forbes.com/sites/forbescoachescouncil/2020/07/17/13-times-in-person-communication-is-better-than-electronic-exchanges/

Cowan, N. (2010). The Magical Mystery Four: How is Working Memory Capacity Limited, and Why? *Current Directions in Psychological Science, 19*(1), 51–57. https://doi.org/10.1177/0963721409359277

Crane, Jacquelyn & Crane, Frederick G. (2010) Optimal Nonverbal Communications Strategies Physicians Should Engage in to Promote Positive Clinical Outcomes, Health Marketing Quarterly, 27:3, 262-274, DOI: 10.1080/07359683.2010.495300

Cullen, M. (2021, May 4). *How to Improve Your Written Communication Skills.* Instructional Solutions. https://www.instructionalsolutions.com/blog/written-communication-skills

Cuncic, A. (2021, July 30). *How to Overcome Eye Contact Anxiety.* Verywell Mind. https://www.verywellmind.com/how-do-i-maintain-good-eye-contact-3024392

Davenport, J. (2021, June 23). *Why Should I Tell a Story?* Duarte. https://www.duarte.com/presentation-skills-resources/why-should-i-tell-a-story/

Davies, E. (2019, April 23). *Change to a learner's mindset.* A Year With My Camera. https://ayearwithmycamera.com/blog/change-to-a-learners-mindset

Dean, B. (2021, March 10). *Zoom User Stats: How Many People Use Zoom in 2022?* Backlinko. https://backlinko.com/zoom-users

Deschene, L. (2014, August 11). *How to Deal with Criticism Well: 25 Reasons to Embrace It.* Tiny Buddha. https://tinybuddha.com/blog/how-to-deal-with-criticism-well-25-reasons-to-embrace-it/

Discover The Power of Voice Inflection in Sales. (2019, September 9). Abstrakt Marketing Group. https://www.abstraktmg.com/driving-leads/from-monotone-to-moving-the-power-of-voice-inflection/

Dlugan, A. (2008, April 10). 10 Ways Your Presentation Skills Generate Career Promotions. *Six Minutes.* http://sixminutes.dlugan.com/career-promotions-presentation-skills/

Doyle, A. (2020, November 24). *Important Active Listening Skills and Techniques.* The Balance Careers. https://www.thebalancecareers.com/active-listening-skills-with-examples-2059684

Duarte, N. (2012a, October 10). Create a Presentation Your Audience Will Care About. *Harvard Business Review.* https://hbr.org/2012/10/create-presentations-an-audien

Duarte, N. (2012b, November 12). Disarm Your Audience When You Present. *Harvard Business Review.* https://hbr.org/2012/11/disarm-your-audience-when-you

Duarte, N. (2018a, April 5). *10 Ways to Prepare for a TED Style Talk.* Duarte. https://www.duarte.com/presentation-skills-resources/10-ways-to-prepare-for-a-ted-format-talk/

Duarte, N. (2018b, July 19). *How to Develop the Best Big Idea for Your Presentation*. Duarte. https://www.duarte.com/presentation-skills-resources/how-to-develop-the-best-big-idea-for-your-presentation/

Duarte, N. (2018c, October 16). *Overcome Presentation Anxiety Easily with These Steps*. Duarte. https://www.duarte.com/presentation-skills-resources/overcome-presentation-anxiety-easily-with-these-steps/

Duarte, N. (2019, June 11). *Use Contrast in the Middle of a Presentation to Transform*. Duarte. https://www.duarte.com/presentation-skills-resources/use-contrast-in-the-middle-of-a-presentation-to-transform/

Effective communication skills for business and personal success—How To Paraphrase. (n.d.). Maximum Advantage: Psychology Applied to Life. http://www.maximumadvantage.com/how-to-paraphrase.html

Efficient Phone Communication | SkillsYouNeed. (n.d.). Skills You Need. https://www.skillsyouneed.com/rhubarb/efficient-phone-communication.html

Elkins, K. (2019, August 30). *Warren Buffett: Developing this skill can make "a major difference in your future earning power."* CNBC. https://www.cnbc.com/2019/08/30/warren-buffett-why-you-should-focus-on-your-communication-skills.html

Elkins, K. (2019, August 30). *Warren Buffett: Why you should focus on your communication skills*. CNBC. https://www.cnbc.com/2019/08/30/warren-buffett-why-you-should-focus-on-your-communication-skills.html

Engel, J. M. (2018, December 19). *How Empathic And Active Listening Can Improve Workplace Communication.* Forbes. https://www.forbes.com/sites/ forbescoachescouncil/2018/12/19/how-empathic-and-active-listening-can-improve-workplace-communication/

Erin Montoya, J. H. (2021, July 6). *'Are crossed arms rude?' Body language expert weighs in on trending topic.* Click2Houston. https://www.click2houston.com/houston-life/2021/07/06/ are-crossed-arms-rude-body-language-expert-weighs-in-on-trending-topic/#:~:text=During%20 negotiations%20it%20typically%20signifies,%2C%20 insecure%2C%20defensive%20or%20anxious.

Essential Business Analyst Skills. (n.d.). *Sharpen Your Communication Skills Unit.* Salesforce Trailhead. Retrieved March 19, 2022, from https://trailhead.salesforce.com/en/content/ learn/modules/business-analyst_skills-strategies/ sharpen-your-communication-skills

Farley, J., Risko, E., & Kingstone, A. (2013). Everyday attention and lecture retention: The effects of time, fidgeting, and mind wandering. *Frontiers in Psychology, 4.* https://www. frontiersin.org/article/10.3389/fpsyg.2013.00619

Finn, M. (2021, October 20). *How to Reduce Stress Like a Navy SEAL.* Gear Patrol. http://gearpatrol.com/fitness/ health-wellness/a325714/box-breathing-navy-seals/

Fischer, A. (2018, October 5). *5 Ways to Use Eye Contact in a Business Meeting to Get What You Want.* Entrepreneur. https://www.entrepreneur.com/article/320497

Forbes Team. (2017, October 30). *Forbes Insights: 5 Reasons Why Your Company Needs to Embrace Video Conferencing Now.* Forbes. https://www.forbes.com/sites/insights-zoom/2017/10/30/5-reasons-why-your-company-needs-to-embrace-video-conferencing-now/?sh=7d50b8ac47c4

Forget "Best" or "Sincerely," This Email Closing Gets the Most Replies. (2017, January 31). *Boomerang: Email Productivity.* https://blog.boomerangapp.com/2017/01/how-to-end-an-email-email-sign-offs/

Furmark, T., Tillfors, M., Everz, P., Marteinsdottir, I., Gefvert, O., & Fredrikson, M. (1999). Social phobia in the general population: Prevalence and sociodemographic profile. *Social Psychiatry and Psychiatric Epidemiology, 34*(8), 416–424. https://doi.org/10.1007/s001270050163

Gallo, C. (2014, September 25). *New Survey: 70% Say Presentation Skills Are Critical For Career Success.* Forbes. https://www.forbes.com/sites/carminegallo/2014/09/25/new-survey-70-percent-say-presentation-skills-critical-for-career-success/

Gallo, C. (2015, July 7). *Richard Branson: "Communication Is The Most Important Skill Any Leader Can Possess."* Forbes. https://www.forbes.com/sites/carminegallo/2015/07/07/richard-branson-communication-is-the-most-important-skill-any-leader-can-possess/

Gershman, S. (2019, September 17). To Overcome Your Fear of Public Speaking, Stop Thinking About Yourself. *Harvard Business Review.* https://hbr.org/2019/09/to-overcome-your-fear-of-public-speaking-stop-thinking-about-yourself

Giang, V. (2021, September 9). *How Can Body Language Project Self-Confidence*. Business Class: Trends and Insights | American Express. https://www.americanexpress. com/en-us/business/trends-and-insights/ articles/4-ways-your-body-language-can-project-confidence/

Glassdoor Team. (2021, June 29). *Active Listening in the Workplace—Glassdoor Career Guides*. Glassdoor. https://www. glassdoor.com/blog/guide/active-listening-definition/

GMAC Research Team. (2020, July 30). *Communication Skills Still Super Important to Employers*. https://www. mba.com/information-and-news/research-and-data/ employers-seek-communications-skills

Goman, C. K. (2018, August 26). *5 Ways Body Language Impacts Leadership Results*. Forbes. https://www.forbes. com/sites/carolkinseygoman/2018/08/26/5-ways-body-language-impacts-leadership-results/

Gomez, S. (2019, February 25). *7 Ways to Increase Your Visibility at Work Before a Performance Review*. Adobe Workfront. https://www.workfront.com/blog/ raise-your-profile-your-visibility-at-work-performance-review

Gottman, J.M. (1994). What Predicts Divorce?: The Relationship Between Marital Processes and Marital Outcomes (1st ed.). Psychology Press. https://doi.org/10.4324/9781315806808

Grammarly Review 2021 (Premium vs Free). (2021, January 3). *Daily Logo Challenge Blog*. https://blog. dailylogochallenge.com/grammarly-review/

Greenley, B. (2017, January 31). *Forget "Best" or "Sincerely,"* *This Email Closing Gets the Most Replies.* Boomerang. https://blog.boomerangapp.com/2017/01/ how-to-end-an-email-email-sign-offs/

Gupta, R., Koscik, T. R., Bechara, A., & Tranel, D. (2011). The amygdala and decision-making. *Neuropsychologia, 49*(4), 760–766. https://doi.org/10.1016/j.neuropsychologia.2010.09.029

Guthrie, S. (2018, March 14). Why Presentation Skills Are the Most Important Skill Set to Have. *Presentation Training Institute.* https://www.presentationtraininginstitute. com/presentation-skills-important-skill-set/

Guthrie-Jensen Consultants. (2013, July 3). Get Your Point Across—Clearly and Confidently. *INSIGHTS: The Guthrie-Jensen Blog.* https://guthriejensen.com/blog/ get-your-point-across-clearly-and-confidently/

Haddock, P. (2020, October 25). Watch Your Tone when Writing and Speaking. *On Being a Writer | Medium.* https://medium.com/on-being-a-writer/ watch-your-tone-when-writing-and-speaking-576d31fc98f2

Handel, S. (2013, February 17). *The Unconscious Influence of Mirroring: The Power of Mimicking Other People's Body Language.* The Emotion Machine. https://www.theemotionmachine. com/the-unconscious-influence-of-mirroring/

Hansen, Jochim & Wänke, Michaela. (2010). Truth From Language and Truth From Fit: The Impact of Linguistic Concreteness and Level of Construal on

Subjective Truth. Personality & social psychology bulletin. 36. 1576-88. 10.1177/0146167210386238.

Harris, G. (2009, October 6). *Effective Communication Skills: Acknowledge Emotions Before Solving Problems.* Guy Harris: The Recovering Engineer. https://recoveringengineer. com/resolving-conflict/effective-communication-skills-acknowledge-emotions-before-solving-problems/

Harrison, A. (2018, January 4). *How to Really Craft Audience-Centric Presentations.* Duarte. https:// www.duarte.com/presentation-skills-resources/ how-to-write-audience-centric-presentation/

Harrison. (2020, June 1). *Mirror verbal and non-verbal communication to build good rapport.* Cutting Edge PR Insights. https:// cuttingedgepr.com/mirror-verbal-and-nonverbal-communication-to-build-rapport/

Hartanto, T. A., Krafft, C. E., Iosif, A. M., & Schweitzer, J. B. (2016). A trial-by-trial analysis reveals more intense physical activity is associated with better cognitive control performance in attention-deficit/hyperactivity disorder. *Child Neuropsychology, 22*(5), 618–626. https:// doi.org/10.1080/09297049.2015.1044511

Heathfield, S. M. (2019, November 30). *The Best Strategies to Raise Your Visibility at Work.* The Balance Careers. https://www.thebalancecareers.com/ how-to-raise-your-visibility-at-work-1919217

Heathfield, S. M. (2020, November 10). *You'll Get More Feedback if You Receive It With Grace and Dignity.* The

Balance Careers. https://www.thebalancecareers.com/
receive-feedback-with-grace-and-dignity-1916643

Heavens-Woodcock, A. (2020, March 26). How to
Communicate Effectively via Video Conferencing.
Digital Hill. https://www.digitalhill.com/blog/
how-to-communicate-effectively-via-video-conferencing/

Hernandez, N. (2020, July 18). Science Says This
Breathing Exercise Will Help You Calm Down
Quickly. *Calm Cuban.* https://calmcuban.com/
science-breathing-exercise-calm-down-quickly/

Hogan, M. (2016, February 8). *5 Employee Feedback Stats That You Need
to See.* LinkedIn. https://www.linkedin.com/business/talent/
blog/talent-strategy/employee-feedback-stats-you-need-to-see

How to Be Confident and Reduce Stress in 2 Minutes Per
Day. (2013, July 25). *James Clear.* https://jamesclear.
com/body-language-how-to-be-confident

How To Build Presentation Structure. (2014, October 2). Duarte.
https://www.duarte.com/building-presentation-structure/

How to Get Better at Making Phone Calls | SkillsYouNeed.
(n.d.). Skills You Need. https://www.skillsyouneed.
com/rhubarb/make-better-phone-calls.html

How to Give and Receive Feedback that Doesn't Suck. (2019,
May 31). Engineers Rising LLC. https://www.
engineersrising.com/blog/feedback

How to Improve Leadership Communication - Use Questions to Create Awareness of New Possibilities &mdash. The Savage Leader. (2022, February 10). The Savage Leader. https://www. thesavageleader.com/journal/leadership-communication-tip-use-questions-to-create-awareness-of-new-possibilities

How to Read Body Language—Revealing Secrets Behind Nonverbal Cues. (2013, April 26). Fremont University. https:// fremont.edu/how-to-read-body-language-revealing-the-secrets-behind-common-nonverbal-cues/

How to take constructive feedback like a boss. (n.d.). Impraise. https://www.impraise.com/blog/how-to-take-constructive-feedback-like-a-boss

Inc Editorial Team. (2020, February 6). *Written Communication—Encyclopedia—Business Terms.* Inc.Com. https://www.inc.com/encyclopedia/written-communication.html

Increasing Your Visibility: Raising Your Profile at Work. (n.d.). Mind Tools. http://www.mindtools.com/pages/article/increasing-visibility.htm

Indeed Editorial Team. (2021a, February 23). *10 Ways To Improve Verbal Communication Skills.* Indeed Career Guide. https:// www.indeed.com/career-advice/career-development/how-to-improve-verbal-communication-skills

Indeed Editorial Team. (2021b, December 6). *Active Listening Skills: A Key To Effective Communication In The Workplace.* Indeed Career Guide. https://ca.indeed.com/career-advice/career-development/active-listening-skills

James, W. (1893). *Psychology.* Henry Holt and Company.

Just Breathe. (2020, November 25). DBH NOW. https://www.dbhnow.org/wellness/just-breathe

Kelly, J. (2019, March 15). *How To Stop Comparing Your Career To Others' And Start Feeling Good About Yourself.* Forbes. https://www.forbes.com/sites/jackkelly/2019/03/15/how-to-stop-comparing-your-career-to-others-and-start-feeling-good-about-yourself/

Kemp, K. (2019, January 10). *Five reasons why pointless meetings can hurt your business.* BusinessInsider. https://www.insider.co.uk/special-reports/doodle-pointless-meetings-brexit-businesses-13833784

Kokemuller, N. (n.d.). *Business Etiquette on Eye Contact.* Small Business - Chron.Com. https://smallbusiness.chron.com/business-etiquette-eye-contact-76161.html

Kramar, E. J. J., & Lewis, T. R. (1951). Comparison of Visual and Nonvisual Listening. *Journal of Communication, 1*(2), 16–20. https://doi.org/10.1111/j.1460-2466.1951.tb00110.x

Kraus, M. W. (2017a). Voice-only communication enhances empathic accuracy. *American Psychologist, 72*(7), 644–654. https://doi.org/10.1037/amp0000147

Kraus, M. W. (2017b, October 10). *Listeners Glean Emotions Better from Voice-Only Communications.* Yale Insights. https://insights.som.yale.edu/insights/listeners-glean-emotions-better-from-voice-only-communications

Krle, E. (2019, March 22). How Eye Contact Can Help You Succeed in Business and Life. *The Good Men Project.* https://goodmenproject.com/guy-talk/how-eye-contact-can-help-you-succeed-in-business-and-life-cmtt/

Kruse, K. (2014, April 12). *How To Receive Feedback And Criticism.* Forbes. https://www.forbes.com/sites/kevinkruse/2014/08/12/how-to-receive-feedback-and-criticism/

Kwik, J.(2020). *Limitless: Upgrade Your Brain, Learn Anything Faster, and Unlock Your Exceptional Life.* Hay House Inc.

Lab, P. W. (n.d.). *Tone in Business Writing // Purdue Writing Lab.* Purdue Writing Lab. https://owl.purdue.edu/owl/subject_specific_writing/professional_technical_writing/tone_in_business_writing.html

Lattice Team. (2019, September 24). *How to Ask Your Manager for Feedback.* Lattice. https://lattice.com/library/how-to-ask-your-manager-for-feedback

Levine, J. A., Eberhardt, N. L., & Jensen, M. D. (1999). Role of Nonexercise Activity Thermogenesis in Resistance to Fat Gain in Humans. *Science.* https://doi.org/10.1126/science.283.5399.212

Levine, J. A., Schleusner, S. J., & Jensen, M. D. (2000). Energy expenditure of nonexercise activity. *The American Journal of Clinical Nutrition, 72*(6), 1451–1454. https://doi.org/10.1093/ajcn/72.6.1451

Locke, R. (2014, July 28). *8 Ways Of Giving Constructive Feedback That Make An Impact.* Lifehack. https://www.lifehack.org/articles/work/8-ways-giving-constructive-feedback-that-make-impact.html

Loudon, I. (2013). Ignaz Phillip Semmelweis' studies of death in childbirth. *Journal of the Royal Society of Medicine, 106*(11), 461–463. https://doi.org/10.1177/0141076813507844

Lowenbraun, N., & Davenport, J. (2020, May 12). *Dynamic Virtual Presentations: How to Stand Out.* Duarte. https://www.duarte.com/presentation-skills-resources/dynamic-virtual-presentations/

Lufkin, B. (2020, April 9). *Five tips to look your best on video calls.* BBC. https://www.bbc.com/worklife/article/20200407-zoom-five-tips-to-look-your-best-on-video-calls

MacGill , M. (2017, September 4). *What is the link between love and oxytocin?* [Press release]. Medical New Today. https://www.medicalnewstoday.com/articles/275795

Magazine, S., & Stromberg, J. (2012, July 12). *Myth Busted: Looking Left or Right Doesn't Indicate If You're Lying.* SmithsonianMag [Magazine]. https://www.smithsonianmag.com/science-nature/myth-busted-looking-left-or-right-doesnt-indicate-if-youre-lying-1922058/

Manson, M. (2021, February 7). *The Levels of Eye Contact.* Mark Manson. https://markmanson.net/the-levels-of-eye-contact

Marmolejo-Ramos, F., Murata, A., Sasaki, K., Yamada, Y., Ikeda, A., Hinojosa, J. A., Watanabe, K., Parzuchowski, M., Tirado, C., &

Ospina, R. (2020). Your Face and Moves Seem Happier When I Smile: Facial Action Influences the Perception of Emotional Faces and Biological Motion Stimuli. *Experimental Psychology, 67*(1), 14–22. https://doi.org/10.1027/1618-3169/a000470

Maslow, A. (n.d.). *You will either step forward into growth or you will step back into safety.* Retrieved March 19, 2022, from https://www.heroic.us/optimize/quotes/abraham-maslow/you-will-either-step-forward-into-growth.

McAleer, P., Todorov, A., & Belin, P. (2014). How Do You Say 'Hello'? Personality Impressions from Brief Novel Voices. *PLOS ONE, 9*(3), e90779. https://doi.org/10.1371/journal.pone.0090779

McNamara, C. (2012, January 26). *Useful Communications Skills—How to Paraphrase and Summarize.* Free Management Library. https://managementhelp.org/blogs/personal-and-professional-coaching/2012/01/26/useful-communications-skills-how-to-paraphrase-and-summarize/

Meah, A., & Al-Jarrah, H. (2018, May 7). *40 Inspirational Tom Bilyeu Quotes On Success.* Awaken The Greatness Within. https://www.awakenthegreatnesswithin.com/40-inspirational-tom-bilyeu-quotes-on-success/

Mohiyeddini, C., Bauer, S., & Semple, S. (2013). Displacement Behaviour Is Associated with Reduced Stress Levels among Men but Not Women. *PLOS ONE, 8*(2), e56355. https://doi.org/10.1371/journal.pone.0056355

Montopoli, J. (2017, February 20). PUBLIC SPEAKING ANXIETY AND FEAR OF BRAIN FREEZES. *National*

Social Anxiety Center. https://nationalsocialanxietycenter.
com/2017/02/20/public-speaking-and-fear-of-brain-freezes/

Moore, E. (2021, December 19). *What to say when you don't know
an answer at work.* Overheard on Conference Calls. https://
overheardonconferencecalls.com/business/what-to-say-
when-you-dont-know-an-answer-to-a-question-at-work/

Moore, K. (2016, April 7). *Study: 73% of Employers Want
Candidates With This Skill.* Inc.Com. https://www.
inc.com/kaleigh-moore/study-73-of-employers-
want-candidates-with-this-skill.html

Morgan, B. (2019, September 24). *50 Stats That Prove The Value
Of Customer Experience.* Forbes. https://www.forbes.com/
sites/blakemorgan/2019/09/24/50-stats-that-prove-
the-value-of-customer-experience/?sh=7622d5f04ef2

Morgan, N. (2018). *Can you hear me? How to connect with people
in a virtual world.* Harvard Business Review Press.

Nazish, N. (2019, May 30). *How To De-Stress In 5 Minutes Or
Less, According To A Navy SEAL.* Forbes. https://www.
forbes.com/sites/nomanazish/2019/05/30/how-to-de-
stress-in-5-minutes-or-less-according-to-a-navy-seal/

Non Verbal Communication, Non Verbal Cues and Skills to
Master. (n.d.). *Tonyrobbins.Com.* https://www.tonyrobbins.
com/personal-growth/nonverbal-communication/

Non-Verbal Communication | SkillsYouNeed. (n.d.). Skills
You Need. https://www.skillsyouneed.com/
ips/nonverbal-communication.html

Nonverbal Communication in Business: 17 Tips to Boost Sales. (2021, July 15). Science of People. https://www. scienceofpeople.com/body-language-business/

Norrish, B. (2021, June 28). *3 Tips To Improve Your Verbal Communication Skills.* Medium. https:// betterprogramming.pub/3-tips-to-improve-your-verbal-communication-skills-d461ff36688a

O'Hara, C. (2015, May 15). How to Get the Feedback You Need. *Harvard Business Review.* https://hbr. org/2015/05/how-to-get-the-feedback-you-need

Orcutt. (2021, January 18). *Techniques for Using Critique Language for More Powerful and Effective Presentations.* Duarte. https://www.duarte.com/presentation-skills-resources/techniques-for-using-critique-language-for-more-powerful-and-effective-presentations/

Patankar, V. (2010, April 26). *Emailing Awesomely – The Definitive Guide to Email Structure.* AL. http://www.abstract-living.com/emailing-awesomely-the-definitive-guide-to-email-structure/

Persuasive Presentations: Story Structure. (2014, April 23). Duarte. https://www.duarte.com/persuasive-presentations-story-structure/

Pinocchio effect': Lying sends nose-tip temperature soaring, but size unchanged: scientist. (2012, November 24). NEW YORK DAILY NEWS. https://www.nydailynews.com/life-style/health/pinocchio-effect-lying-sends-nose-tip-temperature-soaring-scientists-article-1.1206872

PON Staff. (2020, October 8). Negotiation Skills for Win-
Win Negotiations. *PON - Program on Negotiation at
Harvard Law School.* https://www.pon.harvard.edu/daily/
negotiation-skills-daily/listening-skills-for-maximum-success/

Positive Feedback Loops in Early Human Development. (n.d.).
123 Help Me. https://www.123helpme.com/essay/
Positive-Feedback-Loops-in-Early-Human-Development-22194

Pronk, N. P., Katz, A. S., Lowry, M., & Payfer, J. R. (2012).
Reducing occupational sitting time and improving worker
health: The Take-a-Stand Project, 2011. *Preventing Chronic
Disease, 9,* E154. https://doi.org/10.5888/pcd9.110323

Pry, A., & Ahn, J. (2019, February 4). *How to get confident and speak up
at work.* Yahoo! Finance. https://finance.yahoo.com/news/
how-to-get-confident-and-speak-up-at-work-163435420.html

Puder, D. (2018, May 14). *Episode 016: Microexpressions: Fear,
Surprise, Disgust, Empathy, and Creating Connection Part 2 &mdash*
[Podcast]. Psychiatry & Psychotherapy Podcast. https://www.
psychiatrypodcast.com/psychiatry-psychotherapy-podcast/
microexpressions-emotions-empathy

Sayler, S. (2011, February). *Body Language Dos and Don'ts to
Help You Win in the Business World.* New York Society
of Association Executives (NYSAE). https://
www.nysaenet.org/resources1/inviewnewsletter/
archives/20111/february2011/inview22011_article7

Schulz, J. (2012, December 31). *Eye contact: Don't make these mistakes.*
Michigan State University Extension. https://www.canr.
msu.edu/news/eye_contact_dont_make_these_mistakes

Seiter, C. (2018, May 9). *Step-by-Step: How to Give and Receive Feedback at Work*. Buffer Resources. https://buffer.com/resources/how-to-give-receive-feedback-work/

Serlin, E. (2018, July 4). *Why Do We Struggle With Communication At Work?* London Speech Workshop Blog. https://blog.londonspeechworkshop.com/why-do-we-struggle-with-communications-at-work

Shaoolian, G. (2018, February 23). *This Is The Right Way To Ask Your Boss For Feedback*. Fast Company. https://www.fastcompany.com/40534663/this-is-the-right-way-to-ask-your-boss-for-feedback

Shellenbarger, S. (2016, September 20). Use Mirroring to Connect With Others. *Wall Street Journal*. https://www.wsj.com/articles/use-mirroring-to-connect-with-others-1474394329

Shenton, C. (2019, December 3). *How Important is Feedback at Work for Business Success?* Weekly10. https://www.weekly10.com/how-important-is-feedback-in-the-workplace-to-the-success-of-business/

Smith, D. D. (2019, January 17). *Getting Your Voice Into The Room When You're Afraid To Speak Up*. Forbes. https://www.forbes.com/sites/forbescoachescouncil/2019/01/17/getting-your-voice-into-the-room-when-youre-afraid-to-speak-up/

Smith, J. (2013). *10 Nonverbal Cues That Convey Confidence At Work*. Forbes. https://www.forbes.com/sites/jacquelynsmith/2013/03/11/10-nonverbal-cues-that-convey-confidence-at-work/

Spector, N. (2017, November 28). *Smiling can trick your brain into happiness—And boost your health.* NBC News. https://www.nbcnews.com/better/health/smiling-can-trick-your-brain-happiness-boost-your-health-ncna822591

Stjelja, N. (2019, March 30). How to answer question you don't know the answer to. *Medium.* https://medium.com/@nikolastjelja/how-to-answer-question-you-dont-know-the-answer-to-be5d231a1349

Stok, G. (2020, November 29). *Face-to-Face Conversation Is Important for Success.* ToughNickel. https://toughnickel.com/business/How-to-Have-a-Meaningful-Face-to-Face-Conversation

Sullivan, B., & Thompson, H. (2013, May 3). *Now Hear This! Most People Stink at Listening [Excerpt].* Scientific American. https://www.scientificamerican.com/article/plateau-effect-digital-gadget-distraction-attention/

Sullivan, J. (2016). *Simply said: Communicating better at work and beyond.* John Wiley & Sons.

Talking to Customers: Phone vs. Email. (n.d.). Grasshopper. https://grasshopper.com/resources/articles/talking-to-customers-phone-vs-email/

Team Tony. (2015, June 5). Top 10 tips to have more confident body language. *Tony Robbins.* https://www.tonyrobbins.com/mind-meaning/confidence-and-charisma/

Tenser, D. (2021, December 28). *What Is The Subject In An Email?* djst.org. https://djst.org/office/what-is-the-subject-in-an-email/

The Tonight Show Starring Jimmy Fallon: Hashtag Gallery: #TextFail Photo: 3019481 - NBC.com. (n.d.). NBC. https://www.nbc.com/ the-tonight-show/photos/hashtag-gallery-textfail/3019481

Thompson, M. (2020, March 9). *According to Warren Buffett, Honing This One Skill Can Improve Your Worth by 50 Percent.* Medium. https://entrepreneurshandbook.co/ according-to-warren-buffett-honing-this-one-skill-can-improve-your-worth-by-50-percent-9221cd79356

Thorp, A. A., Kingwell, B. A., Owen, N., & Dunstan, D. W. (2014). Breaking up workplace sitting time with intermittent standing bouts improves fatigue and musculoskeletal discomfort in overweight/obese office workers. *Occupational and Environmental Medicine, 71*(11), 765–771. https://doi.org/10.1136/oemed-2014-102348

Toledo, M. (2018, May 30). *Business Tools: The Art Of Listening.* Forbes. https://www.forbes. com/sites/forbeslacouncil/2018/05/30/ business-tools-the-art-of-listening/

Top 10 Tips for Effective Workplace Communication. (2013, May 9). Fremont University. https://fremont.edu/ top-10-tips-for-effective-workplace-communication/

Torgovnick May, K. (2012, October 31). How to give a persuasive presentations: A Q&A with Nancy Duarte | TED Blog. *TED Blog.* https://blog.ted.com/how-to-give-more-persuasive-presentations-a-qa-with-nancy-duarte/

Tschabitscher, H. (2020, March 15). *Want to Write Emails That Are Easier to Read? Try This.* Lifewire. https://www.lifewire.com/bullet-points-in-emails-1165431

Unite Your Presentation Around One Point. (2014, May 20). Duarte. https://www.duarte.com/unite-your-presentation-around-one-point/

Van Edwards, V. (2014, December 8). *10 Steps to Conquering Your Phone Anxiety.* Science of People. https://www.scienceofpeople.com/phone-anxiety/

Van Edwards, V. (2016, September 9). *15 Science-Based Public Speaking Tips To Be a Master Speaker.* Science of People. https://www.scienceofpeople.com/public-speaking-tips/

Van Edwards, V. (2017, November 2). *How to Give Captivating Presentations.* Science of People. https://www.scienceofpeople.com/how-to-give-captivating-presentations/

Van Edwards, V. (2018, September 21). *Stage Fright: How to Overcome It in 7 Easy Steps.* Science of People. https://www.scienceofpeople.com/stage-fright/

Van Edwards, V. (2020a, March 26). *16 Amazing Tips to Look Good on Zoom and Webcam Videos.* Science of People. https://www.scienceofpeople.com/zoom-tips/

Van Edwards, V. (2020b, April 20). *How to Speak with Confidence and Sound Better.* Science of People. https://www.scienceofpeople.com/speak-with-confidence/

Van Edwards, V. (2020c, May 5). *12 Tips to Give an Amazing Online Presentation*. Science of People. https://www.scienceofpeople.com/online-presentation/

Van Edwards, V. (2020d, July 7). *10 Presentation Ideas That Will Radically Improve Your Presentation Skills*. Science of People. https://www.scienceofpeople.com/presentation-ideas/

Van Edwards, V. (2020e, July 7). *How to Start a Speech: The Best (and Worst) Speech Openers*. Science of People. https://www.scienceofpeople.com/how-to-start-a-speech/

Van Edwards, V., & Fonseca, T. A. (2015, August 7). *Mirroring Body Language: 4 Steps To Successfully Mirror Others*. Science of People. https://www.scienceofpeople.com/mirroring/

Verghese, S. (2020, February 9). Finding the Courage to Speak up at Work. *The Startup*. https://medium.com/swlh/finding-the-courage-to-speak-up-at-work-5510e3dd28b9

Voigt, S. (2020, May 14). 4 Ways to Advance Your Written Communication Skills When WFH. *Speexx*. https://www.speexx.com/speexx-blog/written-communication-skills/

Voss, C. (2016). *Never Split the Difference: Negotiating Techniques-Summary Cheat Sheet*. famvestor. https://www.famvestor.com/wp-content/uploads/2019/01/NeverSplitTheDifference-Negotiating-Techniques.pdf

Voss, C., & Raz, T. (2016). *Never split the difference: Negotiating as if your life depended on it*. Random House.

Vozza, S. (2016, October 28). *How To Successfully Respond To A Question You Really Don't Want To Answer.* Fast Company. https://www.fastcompany.com/3064575/how-to-successfully-respond-to-a-question-you-really-dont-want-to-answer

Ward, M., Cain, Á., & Akhtar, A. (2022, January 14). *Career experts shared their top 19 tips for writing a good subject line.* Business Insider. https://www.businessinsider.com/how-to-write-an-email-subject-line-2015-1

What is Mirroring—Meaning of Mirroring in Body Language—Harappa Education. (2020, October 29). Harappa. https://harappa.education/harappa-diaries/what-is-mirroring-in-body-language/

When Written Communication is More Effective. (2018, June 11). IEduNote. https://www.iedunote.com/written-communication

Why We Don't Like Being Told What To Do. (2020, November 17). Cleveland Clinic. https://health.clevelandclinic.org/why-we-dont-like-being-told-what-to-do/

Willis, J., & Todorov, A. (2006). First Impressions: Making Up Your Mind After a 100-Ms Exposure to a Face. *Psychological Science, 17*(7), 592–598. https://doi.org/10.1111/j.1467-9280.2006.01750.x

Wiseman, R., Watt, C., Brinke, L. ten, Porter, S., Couper, S.-L., & Rankin, C. (2012). The Eyes Don't Have It: Lie Detection and Neuro-Linguistic Programming. *PLOS ONE, 7*(7), e40259. https://doi.org/10.1371/journal.pone.0040259

Wolfe, E. (2019, September 10). *Video Conferencing Statistics for 2019*. Lifesize. https://www.lifesize.com/en/blog/video-conferencing-statistics/

Wooll, M. (2022, February 14). *Become a pro at asking for feedback (and receiving it)*. BetterUp. https://www.betterup.com/blog/how-to-ask-for-and-receive-feedback

Zaltman, G. (2003). *How customers think: Essential insights into the mind of the market*. Harvard Business School Press.

Zhang, K. (2013, July 23). *How to Give Constructive Feedback in the Workplace*. Lifehack. https://www.lifehack.org/articles/communication/how-give-constructive-feedback-and-avoid-ugly-confrontations.html

Zielinski, D. (2020, September). *The Power of Body Language*. Toastmasters International. https://www.toastmasters.org/magazine/magazine-issues/2020/sept/the-power-of-body-language